INSIDERS' GUIDE® TO RELOCATION

HELP US KEEP THIS GUIDE UP TO DATE

Every effort has been made by the authors and editors to make this guide as accurate and useful as possible. However, many things can change after a guide is published—phone numbers change, facilities come under new management, etc.

We would love to hear from you concerning your experiences with this guide and how you feel it could be improved and be kept up to date. While we may not be able to respond to all comments and suggestions, we'll take them to heart and we'll also make certain to share them with the authors. Please send your comments and suggestions to the following address:

> The Globe Pequot Press
> Reader Response/Editorial Department
> P. O. Box 480
> Guilford, CT 06437

Or you may e-mail us at:

> editorial@GlobePequot.com

Thanks for your input, and happy travels!

INSIDERS'GUIDE®

INSIDERS' GUIDE® TO
RELOCATION

SECOND EDITION

BEVERLY ROMAN AND JOHN HOWELLS

INSIDERS'GUIDE®

GUILFORD, CONNECTICUT
AN IMPRINT OF THE GLOBE PEQUOT PRESS

INSIDERS'GUIDE®

ISSN: 1545-1399
ISBN: 0-7627-2683-0

Manufactured in the United States of America
Second Edition/First Printing

CONTENTS

PREFACE

So—you are moving! You have the distinction of being among the more than forty-two million individuals in America who will do so this year. You, however, are going to be prepared. Together we are going to turn the challenge of moving (which has been compared with such traumas as the loss of a loved one, death, and divorce) into an experience that will be positive, productive, and enriching. Whether you are moving across town or across the country, by reading the *Insiders' Guide to Relocation,* you are going to learn tried-and-true methods to make the transition easier.

If you are among the hundreds of thousands of people who are familiar with the *Insiders' Guides,* you know that the basic philosophy of the books is to give you significant information about a city from an insider's point of view—like a neighbor talking to a neighbor. This *Insiders' Guide* will provide you with a general relocation reference as a precursor to the *Insiders' Guide* for your next city.

Relocation can be especially stressful when children are involved. Talk about your relocation decision with your children in a way that is appropriate for their age level. Career moves do not mean anything to a child who must leave a best friend, so carefully explain your position and the ways you are going to work together to make this move benefit the whole family. Encourage question-and-answer sessions and address

each child's concerns. By offering information about the new city, you will help your children learn about it and ease their apprehension about moving there. Tell your children how you will involve them in the moving process. It is essential that they believe they are an integral part of the move and significant to a successful family relocation.

No one in my family ever really wanted to move, but after we made the decision, we became determined to make the very best of the situation, and I believe we did. We now have friends scattered from coast to coast, as well as in many cities throughout Europe, and our children have told us that the people and places they came to know expanded their minds and their perspectives.

An unexpected dividend of moving is that there is always something you can contribute to a conversation. Because we drove through or lived in so many cities, when strangers tell me where they are from, I answer with, "Oh, I know that city," or, more than likely, "I lived there."

Don't misunderstand me; I do not believe moving is wonderful, nor do I recommend it as a favorite pastime. But if you are reading this book, you have probably made the decision to move, and now we must tackle the basics of a successful relocation so that you can make the very most of the opportunity. Obviously, I'm not exactly a beginner in the art of moving, and I'm delighted to share with you my experience and insights into the process of successful relocation, which I have detailed in Part II. I wish you the best.

—Beverly Roman

Earlier in my working career, I found myself in a most unusual situation, in which I could easily find employment with just about any daily newspaper, almost anywhere in the United States or Canada. It was a marvelous, exhilarating experience. With my wife and two children, we moved more than a dozen times to accept employment in interesting new communities of our choice. We accumulated a world of experience in voluntary relocation. We were extremely fortunate to enjoy several years of unforgettable travel adventure before finally settling down. Then, only because we felt our children would benefit from a more traditional high school experience, we chose our favorite town and reluctantly mothballed our wanderlust.

About the time our children left the nest, I moved into a new career as a full-time author and freelance writer. Since the only office a writer needs is a computer and an Internet modem, the sole restraint on where a writer lives is a good telephone connection. Not very restrictive, is it? Once again, we were free to choose where to relocate, and when. Maintaining our California home as winter quarters, we made several "second-home" relocations, where we lived seasonally for two to four years at a time, always returning to our California home base during inclement weather. At one point, we had two second homes, one on beautiful Rogue River in Oregon and another on a tropical beach in Costa Rica.

Obviously, I'm not exactly a beginner in the art of moving, and I'm delighted to share with you my experience and insights into the process of successful relocation.

—John Howells

PART I:
THE ABCs OF RELOCATING

EVALUATING YOUR RELOCATION

I f you are moving you may feel over-whelmed and are wondering where to begin. Take heart. This book offers practi-cal, cost-effective, and tried-and-true advice that will help you realize a more successful transition. Among the many topics you will find are how to negotiate home sales; ways to save money during relocation; help for career-interrupted part-ners; methods to find new schools and new doctors; tips to help children and families settle into a new community; and, last but not least, guidance that will help you to make the very most of what can ultimately become an exciting opportunity.

Because I moved so many times, I know that familiarity with a city takes the edge off the final plunge of moving there. I suggest researching the prospective area on the Internet, where you can learn almost anything you want to know about a city, followed by personal visits as often as time and finances permit. While visiting, you can venture into the stores, shopping malls, or places that will be of interest to your family to become familiar with the people and services. It may be hard to believe, but you don't have to move very far to experience a change in cultural climate.

Because moving is such an overwhelm-ing task, you may be wondering just where you're going to begin. The best way to start is by evaluating your personal situa-tion. No one understands how a move will affect you better than you can. Take the time to think about everything that is important to you and your family at this point in your life. Please note that the sig-nificant issues in this book can be further researched through the Web sites listed throughout this book.

COST OF LIVING ANALYSIS

First on the agenda is to do a cost of living analysis. Most people perform a very superficial analysis of the financial impact of moving to another city or state. You won't be among these people if you take the time to factor these next suggestions into your calculations. Begin your analysis by comparing your current living expendi-tures with those of the new community. If you are primarily a two-income family, is it possible that one salary will be deleted (at least temporarily) as a result of the move? Also, do you fully understand the impact of a company-requested relocation? Will this move equate to a career move and ulti-mately more monetary compensation? Or could it simply be a lateral move?

The following resources offer various forms of medical assistance in and around the United States, as well as overseas.

Global Care, Inc., (800) 860-1111

Worldwide Assistance Services, (800) 777-8710

Medic Alert emblems, (800) 763-3428

Other factors to consider are your personal day-to-day living expenses. Will the next area require more travel costs (to see family or friends), higher telephone charges, bigger insurance bills (automobile and medical), or more expensive food and clothing purchases? Will the job benefits change in the new position? And, finally, how is the real estate market? Real estate considerations can be significant. You have to think about all the costs associated with buying and selling a home, plus the expenses of redecorating and/or purchasing furniture. You need to evaluate the costs of homes in the new area by comparing houses by square footage, living space, number of rooms, and other amenities that you require.

You certainly do not want to take a step backward when it comes to lifestyle adjustments or to your standard of living; therefore, if the cost of living is substantially higher in the new city than your present location, and you are making a corporate move, you can discuss compensation with your employer. If your move is not corporate-related, you must be sure you can absorb any differentials on your own.

MEDICAL NEEDS

An often overlooked but most significant consideration is your family's medical needs. Transferring care, providers, and insurance must be well thought out. For instance, consider whether anyone in your family requires special care and whether that care will be available in the prospective city.

Physicians recommend that you and your family have a thorough medical, dental, and, if appropriate, eye examination before you move to a new location. Take stock of your family's medications and consult with your doctors to update all medical files. Incidents that occurred and the treatment performed need to be detailed, along with any test results. Keep doctor, dentist, and pharmacist addresses and telephone numbers, even if you are moving out of the state.

CLOSE-UP

Medical Planning

1. Take along a few months' worth of prescription medications with you and refills to last until you are established with a new doctor.

2. Keep all drugs in their labeled containers with the name, strength, and dosage of the drug, plus the name of the physician and pharmacy.

3. Store medications according to directions.

4. Be aware of the side effects of medications.

5. Know whether certain foods or beverages need to be avoided with a medication.

6. Know whether you should be driving while taking a particular drug.

7. Inquire about specialists necessary for your family before you move.

8. Take along an extra pair of eyeglasses or contact lenses, along with prescriptions.

9. Take along the necessary insurance forms and identification card for all members of your family.

CAREER-INTERRUPTED PARTNERS

Today, most families exist on two incomes. When one spouse relocates for his or her job, the other may face "career interruption"—a job change caused by the relocation. Relocation does not necessarily mean having to give up one of those incomes. With the level of telecommunications that exists today, along with some imaginative thinking, you may be able to continue to work for your present employer in another city. If this is not feasible, then you will need to locate a company where you can continue your same career path or research ways to create a new career.

Please note that in this chapter, the person who is being asked to relocate to a new position is referred to as the "employee," and the individual who is career-interrupted is referred to as "partner." The following advice is directed toward the career-interrupted partners and what they can do to reestablish themselves in a new community. It would be helpful if both partners read this chapter and work together in these efforts, since the bottom line will affect you both.

AVENUES OF ASSISTANCE

Intervention from the employee's company should be your first consideration. Many companies are recognizing the challenges two-income families face; therefore, consider the company relocation manager as your first resource. If the employee asks for assistance early on, provisions can be written into the relocation package. Some ways the employee's company can assist career-interrupted partners include swapping résumés with other companies; assisting with résumé writing, job-search counseling and leads; finding a job within the employee's company or with suppliers or customers; and contracting with a career counselor to help find work in the new area.

Depending on the employee's position or the company's policy, this assistance may not be possible. Whether it is feasible or not, the career-interrupted partner needs to evaluate his or her skills and potential in preparation for the relocation. Subscribing to the Sunday editions of the new town's newspaper will help you become familiar with the hiring climate and types of positions available. You can note which companies are hiring and what major industries are established in your new community. Take into consideration

If you want to use the Internet to learn about your new home, www.usacitylink.com is a comprehensive Web site that lists states and cities and offers information regarding travel, tourism, relocation, and detailed city guides, as well as official and independent city and state Web sites.

CLOSE-UP
Job Search without a College Diploma

If you do not possess a college degree, you will find suggestions for other job options from a pamphlet entitled "High Earning Workers Who Don't Have a Bachelor's Degree." This publication lists numerous occupations requiring less than a college degree. To search on your computer, type "Federal Consumer Information Center" into any search engine on the Web. This site lists pamphlets on career training, employment, interview advice, health benefits, jobs of tomorrow, and more. The strategic plan that follows may give you insight to reevaluate your skills, strengths, and interests.

CareerJournal.com is a free site. Its main page highlights the day's top stories, as well as Find A Job and JobAlert features. By using the navigational table of contents down the left-hand side of the screen, you can link to an extensive collection of editorial content, databases, and other services throughout the site.

For information on business start-ups, you will find a wealth of information at SCORE on the Web at www.score.org. SCORE assists entrepreneurs primarily free of charge.

the types of positions you see most frequently advertised. Consider which of these are growth industries, and investigate the financial health of local companies.

You can also find almost every city newspaper on the Internet, but you will get more of a "flavor" of the city by reading the hard copy.

Real estate agencies or the buyer agent that you contact to buy your new home can be another good resource for job information. Look for a firm that either has a good in-house "Partner Career Assistance Program" or can steer you to one of many independent career counselors or strategists. Since spousal reemployment is a major concern, many agencies now offer this service. The relocation staff researches the job market pertinent to the specific field and frequently submits résumés. Some may even assist in arranging interviews before the partner arrives for the first house-hunting trip.

Your university or college alma mater is still another option. Typically, most have career placement offices that offer free career counseling to alumni. Contact the counselor at your former institution by telephone or look on the Internet because most are online. If you no longer live near the school, you can request a telephone interview. Some offices will also put you in contact with other graduates who live in your prospective geographic area and may be able to assist you with networking endeavors.

Career or vocational counselors can be found in the Yellow Pages under "Career," "Employment," or "Vocational." These individuals will assist you with contacts within your field or assess your marketable skills for a possible career change. Their services also include networking (their fingers are on the pulse of the local job market) and help to refine cover letters, résumés, and interviewing skills. They can also generate many ideas and resources, as well as serve as coaches and motivators throughout the job search process.

The Internet is the twenty-first century's best tool for searching for almost anything. Many online services offer career forums, where you can search for information about jobs in the area to which you are moving. In the forums you may find job listings by geographical area and job descriptions. Some keywords to use to find listings are "job," "classifieds," "career," and the area to which you are moving. There are also blank form letters to help you complete your résumé, cover letter, and reference letters.

A PERSONAL STRATEGIC PLAN

Relocating can have an unexpected "upside" for career-interrupted partners. This may be a prime opportunity to reassess professional goals. Ask yourself whether you really want to continue on the same career path; if not, this may be your chance to change or redirect your career, establish a business, or write that book you always wanted to do.

Begin with a thorough personal assessment. Ask yourself questions such as, What are my transferable skills and accomplishments?, What are my talents, and what do I enjoy doing?, and What are some of my successes and how did I achieve them? Then think about how you can use all of this information to create or further a new career.

If you decide to seek another position, you need to compose an eye-catching, targeted, and accomplishment-filled résumé. Electronic résumé databases can help with a job search. These databases classify, code, store, retrieve, and transmit a group of résumés entered into the system, allowing companies to sort résumés by occupation, specialty skills, and location preference in seconds. Employers can access databases whenever needed from almost anywhere in the world to search for qualified candidates. Check at reference desks of public or college libraries for these services, many of which are free. Most services do not sell names for use as mailing lists, but it is good to ask.

Research your new community, keeping in mind your personal and professional goals. An *Insiders' Guide* to your new city will tell you about some of the local businesses. Think about the current needs within the community, the types of professional opportunities, new businesses, or freelance services and/or consultants.

Finally, if you are rusty in the job interview department, be sure to prepare yourself for standard interview questions. Ask a friend to assist you with a mock question-and-answer session and practice your responses. As you do this, think about your mannerisms and overall demeanor. Practicing will help you to feel less nervous when you actually are in an interview situation. Three questions typically used in job interviews are, What can you bring to our company?, Why should we hire you?, and What are your strengths and weaknesses?

In the new community you will need information on job opportunities, as well as help in developing professional contacts. Tap every resource available because you cannot underestimate the job-search process. Tell everyone you meet that you are job hunting and be specific about what you are looking for. You never know who may know of a position.

THE "NOT-SO-AVERAGE" MOVING SCENARIOS

The majority of people who relocate are between the ages of 31 and 40, are married with a working spouse, and have one or two children. However, there are other relocation scenarios that involve unique challenges; these include retirees, individuals with disabilities, and those who shoulder elder care responsibilities. This chapter offers guidance primarily for the latter two.

More and more, retirement and relocation really do go together. If you are retiring and considering moving to a warmer climate, want to be closer to your children's family, or hope to own a home with less maintenance and/or lower taxes, you should carefully evaluate any new location. If your move should prove unsatisfactory, relocating again is not only expensive but also a challenge you surely do not need at this time in your life. For more information about relocating for retirement, see the chapters in Part II.

INDIVIDUALS WITH DISABILITIES

If you or someone in your family is among the disabled population, your moving preparation will need special consideration. Before you move, think about what you or your family member requires in the form of floor plans, handrails, walkways, outside ramps, doorway openings, and work accommodations. Next, research the facilities and extended services that will be available in the new community. Begin your search by contacting the organization that represents you or your family member's specific needs, such as associations for the blind or victims of specific diseases. These organizations can offer advice for finding appropriate medical care and any other special services in the city you are considering. You should also inquire about the move when you contact these organizations. Their personnel and/or your physicians should be able to guide you in smoothing the actual physical move for you or your disabled family member to the new home. Basically, you need to evaluate everything that you or your relative requires well in advance of the move. See the Close-Up in this chapter for other resources to assist you with your planning.

Before your pre-move visit to the new city, contact the association or society for your particular needs and ask about hotels and motels that can accommodate special needs, as well as other travel requirements. These organizations also provide information about other user-friendly facilities, such as places of worship, post offices, museums, banks, and restaurants. When you are making hotel reservations, be sure to mention your requirements so there is a convenient and safe room available for you to have easy access to an exit if an emergency arises.

During your visit, look for special housing, transportation services, restaurants, and hotels that will accommodate your special needs. If you do not locate the services or accesses you require, contact the local township authority. The Americans With Disabilities Act (ADA) has made people very aware of the special needs of people who have disabilities. If ramps do not exist in your new community, you can be instrumental in having some installed by making township officials aware of the existing need.

The moving company you choose will play a significant role in a successful transition, so mention your special needs when you call to set up an appointment. When the representative arrives, further explain your specific needs so that on moving day they will understand the layout and general logistics of your homes, the one you are departing, as well as the one you are moving into. All requirements for special moving care should be understood before moving day. For instance, tell movers what equipment will have to be moved as well as the care that it requires. The company should be aware of equipment such as ceiling-mounted pull-ups that have to be dismantled in preparation for moving day. If the moving company does not perform this service, it can arrange for an outside firm to do the work. All equipment should be dismantled before the actual moving day to avoid adding more confusion to an already busy day. Remember, the more information that the mover has, the easier

and faster the moving day activities will proceed.

ELDER CARE

If you are moving and are among the group of individuals who is presently caring for an aging relative in your home or arranging for his or her care, you have to carefully evaluate the situation well in advance of your relocation.

First of all, consider whether your relative prefers to move with you, or if he or she wants to remain in the current community. If your relative moves with you, you have to think about issues such as the logistics of your new home and whether your relative can safely and comfortably settle in so that you and your family can maintain some privacy. Also consider issues such as your elder's activities, how he or she will meet people of similar age, medical care, and insurance coverage. Basically, think about everything your relative now enjoys and whether it will be available in the new community, and, if not, what alternatives you will have.

If your relative prefers not to move with your family, you need to prepare for dependable assistance and schedule routine check-up visits into your time off from work. Think about not only your relative's condition now but also what could possibly take place in the next few years. Then make a mental checklist for your routine visits. Think about evaluating aspects such as, Do friends call often?, Is your relative driving safely?, Is the refrigerator well stocked?, Does this person appear happy?, and Is his/her home well cared for?

If your relative is frail but living independently, a few simple safeguards can ease anxiety and avert crisis. Household safety checks and "personal emergency response systems" that send distress signals when an elder can't reach the phone

Check your local library reference desk for more information about legal advice, advocacy groups, and resources for people who are disabled or require elder care assistance. You can also type the keywords "disabilities and assistance" or "elder and care" in any search engine on the Internet.

CLOSE-UP
Additional Resources

For elder care: *The Complete Eldercare Planner* by Joy Loverde offers professional advice for families with elder care responsibilities. The planner includes
checklists, communication techniques, a "Documents Locator," record-keeping
forms, questions to ask, and more. Call (312) 642–3611 or visit the Web site
www.elderindustry.com.

The National Association of Area Agencies on Aging manages the Eldercare Locator, a toll-free resource line that helps seniors and their families find
home- and community-based services, including home-delivered meals, transportation, adult day care, legal assistance, and home health services. Call the
Eldercare Locator at (800) 677–1116 or visit the Web site at www.eldercare.org.
This program is funded by the U.S. Department of Health and Human Services.

For individuals with disabilities: Disability and Business Technical Assistance
Centers (DBTACs) offer information, materials, technical assistance, or training
on the Americans With Disabilities Act. Call (800) 949–4232; your call will
automatically be routed to the DBTAC in your region. You can access information via the Internet at www.adata.org/dbtac.html.

The Administration for Children and Families (ACF), within the Department
of Health and Human Services, is responsible for federal programs that pro-
mote the economic and social well-being of families, children, individuals, and
communities. ACF has a strong commitment to working with people with
developmental disabilities, refugees, and migrants to address their needs,
strengths, and abilities. Visit the Web site at www.acf.hhs.gov/acfabout.html.

are among the options. Find a neighbor or
friend who can routinely check on your relative and report back to you.

If you would like to make sure that your
elder is eating right, check into the local
Meals on Wheels program. Each program is
independently run, but basically they all
provide hot lunches and reheatable dinners
that are delivered straight to the home. The
cost is usually minimal and varies from one
agency to another. This effort serves two
purposes: A hot nutritious meal is provided, and there is daily contact with the
elder to ensure that he or she is safe.

A KID'S-EYE VIEW

Studies show that children who move more often have increased difficulty in making friends and finding recreational activities, and they tend to fight more with their parents and siblings compared with children who seldom or never move. These observations are merely an awareness-builder for parents. There are many ways you can make the moving process easier for your children and strive to avoid angry feelings about the transition.

This chapter is organized in two sections. The first section is advice for parents. The second section, which starts with "Moving Tips for Kids," is written specifically for children. Please review "Preparing for Relocation" and "After the Move" and then read through "Moving Tips for Kids," "Survival Boxes," and "Safety Tips" with your children.

PREPARING FOR RELOCATION

Begin by being open and honest about the move and why you believe the relocation is the best choice for your family. Listen when your children verbalize their feelings. Then get them involved in the planning and decisions of the move, as appropriate for their ages. Ask them to clean out their closets and plan the decorations for their new bedrooms. Children tend to worry less when they have something productive to accomplish. It is most important that your children believe that they are being considered in the moving process and that they

are an integral part of achieving a successful move.

If your children express concerns about leaving their friends (and if the distance is not too great), you can arrange for them to have exchange visits during the summer or on a school break. Encourage your children to write to their friends and suggest an occasional phone call on weekends, when the telephone rates are lowest. These efforts will ease the transition from old friendships to new ones.

Children long for security, safety, continuity, and the simple assurance that all will be well. It can be very difficult for a child to leave the familiar and known aspects of their lives. You need to take special care in preparing them and talking to them as much as possible about the advantages of the new location.

If you can take your children with you on your pre-move visit to the new city, it will ease their fears and apprehensions about the area. By all means on this trip, visit the school, and if you have time, visit some of the highlights of the city. If this is

Set an example for your children and join community activities and meet new people. If they see you making these efforts, they will be more apt to do the same. You will all feel better and meet new people along the way.

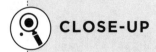
Just for Kids

1. Clean out your toys or things that you have outgrown. If your parents have a garage sale, you can put these items in the sale.

2. Remember—don't throw away anything that has a special meaning.

3. If you are able to go with your mother or father on their pre-move trip to your new city, be sure to visit your new school as well.

4. Try to meet your teachers before the first day of school and get acquainted with them.

5. Check out the new school's bus schedules, activities, and lunch routines.

6. Ask to see your new rooms so you can find them on your first day.

Ask your parents what you can do to help with the packing and other chores that moving requires and write down what you can manage. One thing you might be able to do is to take care of your family pet. Moving is hard on animals as well. You can do a lot to reassure your pet during the moving process. You can also help your parents on moving day by offering to take charge of your pet and keep it safe while the movers are packing. Think about everything your pet needs, such as food and water, daily walks, time to play, brushing, and grooming, and try to help your parents with whatever you can manage. Movers leave doors open while loading furniture, and animals can wander outside and be harmed or lost. So keep your pet in a confined area or on a leash to avoid an accident.

not possible, help your children to learn about the new area as much as possible to ease their entry into the community.

Moving is never easy, but if children are handled with care, the move can be perceived as a positive endeavor. Acknowledge both happy and sad feelings in your children, then show them ways you will work together as a team to make this transition a growing experience for the whole family.

AFTER THE MOVE

When you are in your new home, be sure you make an extra effort to continue family traditions and celebrations. This is an excel-

lent way to maintain continuity in your lives and will help both you and your children feel more secure and comfortable in your new environment.

Remember that no one knows your children better than you do. Pay close attention to changes in your children's daily habits, attire, and attitudes. Following are several signs that can indicate children are struggling in their new environment and ways you can address these.

Some signs that indicate a child is upset are sudden reading difficulties, as well as changes in attention span, eating habits (leading to weight loss or gain), study habits, enthusiasm, energy levels, relationships with you or siblings, and sleep patterns. Teachers may not witness the trouble signs that you see at home; therefore, it is important to communicate any difficulties to them.

Visit the new school and your children's teachers after several weeks to ensure that the adjustment is going well. If you notice any of the above changes in your children, this would be a good time to talk to the teachers about them. Teachers encounter new students so often that they are usually willing and able to help newcomers adjust. You can also seek the assistance of the school guidance counselor if you are especially concerned.

Be sensitive to your own feelings as you prepare for this move. Remember, whatever you are feeling, your children will experience at a magnified level. Loss and change at any age is difficult. Reinforce the fact that you are going to make the move become a positive experience for the whole family. Ultimately, that is what it can become.

Allow your children time to adjust. Sometimes it is better to sort out a new and different situation and new friends and then become selectively involved in the school and the community.

MOVING TIPS FOR KIDS

The idea of going to a new home and school can be very hard and it is only natural if you are concerned about leaving your friends. To keep in touch, plan to exchange letters or e-mails with your friends, and you can also talk to your parents about being able to call a friend or two on weekends. Ask your parents to help you to write down your friends' names, addresses, e-mail addresses, and telephone numbers before you move.

Be sure to talk to your parents about the way you feel about moving. Sometimes

Children's identity is partly formed by feeling at ease in a social group. Help teens to join groups where they might find other newcomers such as exchange students.

when we feel lonely, we want to keep all our feelings inside—please don't do this. The best idea is to talk to your mother or father about your concerns and then plan ways together that will make the move become a nice experience for the whole family.

A fun activity that will help you be a little more excited about the move is to plan your new bedroom. If you know the measurements of your new room, with help from your parents, you can make a practice layout of the room and draw in your bedroom furniture. You can also think about the colors you want to use and easy ways to decorate your room. Fun things to use are posters from school, activities, or your favorite cartoon or movie star. If you have a few ideas you want to use to decorate, write them down and talk them over with your parents.

SURVIVAL BOXES

A survival box can be a small box, a bag, or a backpack. The size of your box may depend on whether you are driving or flying to your new home. You can fill your survival box with the items for your moving trip. These items would be anything that you need during your trip or as soon as you arrive in the new city.

Whenever you move to a new city, it's good to pack a special box in case the moving truck is delayed. Even if the truck arrives on time, sometimes it isn't possible to find the things you need in the hundreds of moving boxes.

Children who are younger may want to fill their survival boxes with favorite stuffed toys or games that they want to take with them to the new house. Older children may want to put in items they will need right away, such as school supplies.

When you plan the activities for your trip to your new home, think about games that do not have a lot of pieces or would be hard to play in a moving car or on an airplane. Board games with magnetic pieces are good for travel. A few fun pastimes for travel are finding cars with a certain description, counting moving trucks, or playing "I Spy" something of a certain color or size.

SAFETY TIPS

Safety in a new community is very important. These tips are to ensure that your experience within your new city is a safe and positive one. The following points will be very important for you to know and remember.

Whenever you travel into any strange location, know your complete name and both your parents' full names as well. It is always important to stay very close to your parents and family, especially in crowded areas.

If you will be temporarily staying in a hotel, know the name and telephone number of your hotel. Other good ideas are to carry a hotel brochure with you, or a map that has the hotel circled on it. Keep a list of phone numbers of friends whom you can call if you should become lost or separated from your family. Write down family names, telephone numbers, and addresses, as well as the new office telephone numbers for your parents. Also be sure that you know your new school bus number and exactly where the bus stop is located. It is a very good idea to do several practice runs from your new home to your bus stop and back before the first day of school to help you remember your new route.

Good luck. Have a wonderful move, stay safe, meet lots of friends, and enjoy your new home.

Try not to complain about the move in front of your children. They are looking to you for reinforcement that everything will be all right.

ORGANIZING YOUR MOVE

This chapter offers you some practical and cost-saving tips that will work for any move. In addition to these tips, start writing down everything that comes to mind in the way of errands, people to call, or chores to be accomplished for your move. The suggestions and lists in this book will help you to remember many small details to achieve an organized and smooth move. To begin, the two key elements in your pre-move organization are household inventories and furniture measurements. These efforts are going to prove invaluable as you proceed through the moving process.

HOUSEHOLD INVENTORY

Having a comprehensive inventory of your household goods makes very good sense whether you are moving or not. To adequately insure your personal belongings during a move, you need to update your inventory with current replacement values. This will enable you to fully insure your belongings during the transportation to your new home.

Insurance is discussed in more detail in the Insurance, Finance, and Estate Guidelines chapter. For now, you need to know that if you do not place a valuation on your goods for the move, the moving company personnel will have to estimate its value. Needless to say, estimates for china, silver, or other valuables could be off the mark if the manufacturers, styles, and other signifi-

cant details are not taken into account. It is important to document your household goods by snapshots or a video camera. Travel through your home using the camera or camcorder and note all furniture, jewelry, and valuables. If you have antiques or items of unusual worth, you will need proof of their value (such as a jeweler's or antiques dealer's estimated value form). Now is the time to get started on this chore because it will take time and effort on your part to collect the necessary appraisals and/or replacement values for your belongings.

MEASURING YOUR FURNITURE

The second most useful exercise for a move is measuring your furniture. Do this before you start looking at homes so you can take the measurements with you. Each time you survey a room in a prospective home, you will know whether or not the furniture will fit in the rooms. As a result, you will not buy a home that will not accommodate your bedroom furniture.

You can purchase a ready-made home kit, referred to as a "template," from an office supply store to measure your furniture. This is a premade version of the method outlined in this chapter, and although it saves some work, it does not always include all your furniture sizes.

CLOSE-UP

Organizational Lists

Notify the following of your change of address before you move. Add whatever is relevant to your family and keep the lists, updating as necessary. Should you move again, it will give you a good base to add to as needed.

Address Changes

Driver's license
Car registration
Voter registration
Magazines and periodicals (allow 6 to 8 weeks)
Charge accounts/department stores
Insurance companies
Investments
Stockbroker
College bursar's offices
Finance companies/car loan
Bank
Airline frequent-flier cards
Family/friends
Organizations/clubs

Final Billings

Telephone companies
Electric company
Gas company
Oil company
Dry cleaner
Newspaper
Tax collector
Trash collector
Recycling company
Water/sewer service
Cable television service
Lawn service

Also, if you should venture into building a home, these measurements will again prove very valuable.

The following is an overview of a quick and easy way to create a plan for each room in your new home. This plan not only guarantees that your furniture will fit in the home, but it also provides a visual map of furniture placement for the movers.

Begin furniture measuring by gathering a yardstick, a tape measure, a pad of paper, a pencil, and a willing assistant. Allow approximately one hour to complete the task, and measure all your furniture room by room. Write down the name of the room, the piece of furniture, and the measurements of the furniture's height, width, and depth.

At this point you need to cut scale models of your furniture from pieces of sturdy paper. Three-by-five-inch cards work well. Purchase graph paper and draw your new rooms to scale ($\frac{1}{4}$ inch equals 1 foot). Make sure that you include the placement of windows, closets, and doors in your drawings.

You can now fit the furniture into the respective rooms on the graph paper, moving the pieces around until you make the most efficient use of the space. Then simply outline your final arrangement on the graph paper. On moving day you can place a plan in each room and tape a number or name to each door.

Unusually large pieces of furniture, such as a piano or dining room table, may require an extra step. In addition to measuring and drawing the piece, you can cut a pattern for it from an old bed sheet. This pattern can be taken with you as you look for a new house and laid out on the floor to give a visual concept of the space the piece will consume.

If you have ever been the only person home on moving day, you will know that having a room plan in each room and naming the rooms eliminates the necessity of putting on your track shoes and running all over the house each time the movers ask, "Where does this belong?" With your room plots and numbers in place, you will simply smile and say, "Use the plan in room three upstairs."

GARAGE SALES

A garage sale is a good way to clear your home of unwanted items, have less to unpack at your destination, and make a little cash in the bargain. Begin by choosing a convenient weekend when you will have the assistance of one or several family members. It is more fun and less costly to have a sale with a few neighbors. Multiple-family sales provide a greater variety of goods to attract customers and allow a sharing of advertising expenses and work.

After picking your days (Fridays and Saturdays are best), go through your home room by room, closet by closet, deciding what items you are never going to need again. Items that have been in the back of a closet and have not seen the light of day

in years probably should be contributed. Gathering items is also a good chore for children. They can select toys, puzzles, and games that they believe they are too old for or that they no longer use. Older children also can assist you in the labeling and pricing of the items for the sale.

Items that sell well are jewelry, furniture, lamps, tools, appliances, books, puzzles, and sports equipment. Clothing does not generally move quickly, with the exception of jeans, jackets, belts, and unusual articles of clothing, including "period" or antique items.

If you are selling lots of plant containers, they will be more attractive and sell faster if you fill them with flowers. An economical flat of flowers will serve the purpose and add color to your sale as well.

One way to speed the pricing chore is to use different colored dots on the items. Red can equal 50 cents, yellow 75 cents, and so on. Make several color charts to tell people the codes and place these around your selling space.

When you price items, you must think "garage sale." The price you put on an item cannot be gauged by what it would garner in a store. Garage sale prices depend on condition, age, and popularity (the lava lamp might sell but the green shag carpet probably won't). If you have never had a garage sale, visit several, or ask an experienced friend for advice before you do your pricing.

Make sure you have plenty of change and one-dollar bills before you begin. If you do not have someone to watch the money box all day, wear an apron or something

CLOSE-UP
Garage Sale Tips

1. When you place your ad in the newspaper, ask if the paper offers garage sale kits. These usually contain signs, balloons, and tags.
2. Clean, wash, and spruce up the sale items as needed before setting them out. Clean items sell better than dirty ones.
3. Place all books, CDs, and videos on desks where they can be easily reached. Most people dislike bending over to forage through boxes, which is how sellers commonly display them. Arrange containers so titles can be read as easily as possible.
4. Keep a sharp eye on valuable items, such as jewelry and coins. Shoplifting can happen at garage sales.
5. If you have things for sale inside the house, post a sign announcing it. Make sure that you or a friend accompanies whoever goes into your home.
6. When selling furniture, try not to break up a set. If someone wants just one item of a set, tell him or her you might consider it toward the end of the sale if the items have not sold as a set.

with pockets to hold the change. Also, be sure to have bags and boxes on hand for people who make large purchases.

The advertisement for the garage sale should run in the daily newspaper on both days of the sale. Take advantage of free advertising, such as bulletin boards in grocery stores and diners, the local "penny saver," or wherever garage sale mavens look. If you live near a college or university, place signs in the student lounges and on bulletin boards. Always mention key items, such as tools, televisions, toys, telephones, or answering machines. On the day of the sale, post signs at busy intersections and significant areas near your home to guide people to the house; note the date of the sale so people will know the sign is current. You should also remove these signs after the sale is over.

If you have leftover items, charitable organizations are usually willing to pick up whatever they think they can use or sell. Most organizations will give you a receipt that you can use when you file your income tax.

Of course, you want to make money on your garage sale. But of equal importance is the money you will save on moving costs. Fewer items to ship means fewer boxes and less wrapping paper, fewer moving hours, a lighter load, and perhaps a smaller truck.

If you are moving a long distance, the cost of the move is based principally on the weight of the load. So take a close look at those older, bulky items in your household. The money you make selling that old refrigerator and the lower cost in moving can be applied to a newer, more energy-efficient model at your new home.

Ask your utility service for a credit reference to use at your next location. You may be able to avoid or lessen your deposit.

PET CORNER

Yes, pets are part of the family, too. Keep your pet in mind during the moving process. Pets can become confused and frightened by unusual activity and increased anxiety just as much as humans. You will have enough to be concerned about during your move; you don't want to worry about your pet getting lost, being injured, or having an accident.

During one of our moves our cat became so frightened of the movers she disappeared at 9:00 P.M. on a rainy night. We finally found her—much later. After this experience we learned to either keep our pets on a leash or harness or confine them to a kennel or small, safe area until we were ready to depart.

Before you leave your old home, make an appointment with your veterinarian to have your pet examined. Vaccinations should be up to date (especially rabies).

Ask your vet for a reference for the new city. A business colleague, a neighbor, or the Yellow Pages in your telephone directory in the new community can be resources to locate pet care. We usually asked someone we came to know who obviously cared very much for his or her pets for a reference.

If your pets have difficulty traveling, ask your veterinarian if a medication is appropriate. Air travel should be booked four weeks ahead of your departure date to ensure convenient travel times. When you book the air travel, you can ask about the airline's regulations for medication and travel. If you are moving in the summer, try to arrange nonstop flights during the early morning or evening hours because it will be cooler.

On moving day and again when you arrive at your new home, contain your pet in a small area, a portable kennel, or a travel case. Confinement will help to

CLOSE-UP
Pet Considerations

1. If you have one or more pets, consider booking a reservation and boarding them in a kennel while the movers are packing. Pets can become confused, difficult, lost, or ill during this time. Your pets will be one less detail to worry about if they are safely ensconced in a kennel until you are ready to depart.
2. When booking a lodging reservation, be sure the hotel or motel allows pets. AAA tour guides have a complete list of hotels and motels that accommodate pets. Also check your local bookstore for travel guides that mention pets.
3. Before crossing into another state, know that some states have border inspections for animals. Contact the state veterinarian's office to learn the rules and regulations.
4. Limit feeding a pet to once a day, preferably in the evening, during your move unless your veterinarian instructs otherwise.
5. The appropriate size for a portable kennel should allow your pet to be able to stand up, lie down, and turn around in natural positions.
6. If you are moving locally, take your pets on several visits to the new home before you move in to familiarize them with their new habitat.
7. Never leave your pets alone in a hot car.

eliminate accidents in unfamiliar surroundings. Be sure your cat knows the new area for the litter box. After all the movers leave, slowly allow your pet more freedom to roam. Always take your dog or cat out with a leash or harness in a new area. Animals have been known to travel thousands of miles to return to their old, familiar homes. Feathered and other pets require special care as well. Your veterinarian or personnel at a good local pet store should have information for travel.

Just as humans thrive on consistency for comfort, so do animals. Try to keep the same routines for your pets, especially mealtimes and walks. Take along the pet's same dishes and bed (no matter how ratty it looks). Familiar beds, bowls, blankets, and toys are soothing to animals.

Don't be alarmed if your pets sleep a lot during the first few days in a new home. This behavior is a normal reaction to change. Your pets are a very important part of your family. By being aware of and reacting to their needs, you can ensure a pleasant moving experience for them, as well as for your entire family.

NEGOTIATING A PROFITABLE HOME SALE

This chapter contains advice to help you make a swift and profitable home sale. There are relatively few people in this world who can afford two mortgages at one time, so before you venture into home buying, your first priority is to sell your home fast, but without losing money.

PRICING YOUR HOME RIGHT— THE FIRST TIME

Profitable home sales begin with realistic pricing. Pricing your home to sell is extremely important because homes that are priced too high at the outset discourage buyers, and the seller can end up realizing 10 percent to 20 percent less on the sale. Ask your real estate agent (preferably someone with selling experience in your area) for an estimate, or you can obtain an appraisal from an appraisal service listed in the Yellow Pages. Be sure that whoever appraises your home is aware of additions and improvements that can easily place your home head and shoulders above neighboring ones. Professionals can validate a price, but you can also check on recent sales for similar neighborhood homes. To learn more about home sales in your neighborhood, visit your county government office and ask for the list of home sales in your area. Deeds to homes are public record, and although there may be a small fee for photocopies, this list will help you learn if your price is reasonable.

If you have the competition of new construction in your area, you will need to factor this into your pricing equation. Consider that resales usually occur at prices below those for new construction, and buyers will choose a resale over new construction only if it is priced right.

The next critical element for a profitable sale is presenting your home in picture-perfect condition. Real estate agents claim that buyers make the decision to purchase a home within the first twenty minutes of viewing it, and the first thing they see is the outside. Don't underestimate curb appeal because many people drive by a home before they make an appointment to see it. Be sure your lawn and gardens are well maintained and look inviting; add flowers, especially around front walks and the entryway. Store all bicycles, toys, and garden tools and have the house number clearly visible. Finally, clean, repair, and/or paint the house, shutters, screens, mailbox, and flower boxes. A suggestion is to walk around the outside of your home and view it from the street as though seeing it through a stranger's eyes.

When prospective buyers step inside your home, they should experience a clean and pleasant environment. Be sensitive to the areas that can harbor unpleasant odors, such as those from pets or a family member who smokes. Allow your agent and buyer some privacy. Try to have the fewest number of family members (and pets) present when a buyer is viewing your home. Be available for questions, but don't travel through the home unless you are asked to do so. Have all the home's records (such as yearly costs for electricity and heating) available. Create an orderly appearance everywhere in your home. Consider bathrooms, closets, basements, attics, and kitchen counters. Clean all appliances that will remain with the home and provide appropriate literature for these appliances. Organize closets and storage areas and basically keep your home "ready to show" as much as possible.

If you are required to move during what is considered the "off-peak" moving season (October to May), don't be discouraged. There are pros and cons to selling a home at any time of the year. The positive aspect of selling an existing home during the off-peak season is that there is less competition during these months, and house hunters at this time are usually serious buyers.

Costs to the seller vary by your state of residence, your personal circumstances, the buyer, and the real estate agency. Costs usually involved are real estate commissions, escrow fees, documentation preparation, recording, notary, title search, insurance, legal fees, and transfer taxes. Depending on the local laws, you might have to provide surveys, home inspections, and some necessary home repairs before you sell the house. Remaining charges to utility companies and other services will be deducted from your deposit, and the balance of deposit returned to you. You should also arrange reimbursement for any prorated refunds on prepaid service contracts, such as exterminators or lawn care.

When you finally get to the magic moment of closing on your home, be sure to hire a real estate attorney and finalize

your bank transfers and mortgage arrangements. Adjust your homeowner's insurance by deleting the old home (if it is sold) and covering the new home. It is important to understand all the closing costs and have a cashier's or bank check prepared for your closing amount. If you are changing mortgage companies, contact the former company—make sure it arranges to close your old account and ask if it requires copies of paperwork for its files. After all the papers are signed, arrange to have the deed recorded.

RENOVATING YOUR HOME FOR SALE

If you are preparing your home for sale and believe you need to renovate to improve its salability, here are points to help you to realize a financially sound investment. Think about the age of your home and whether it will easily lend itself to the remodeling. Consider whether the renovations you are planning are minor or major, how much time the changes will require, and if you can stay in the home while the work is being done. Also, consider how much of the basic structure will remain unchanged, and calculate whether changes will cost more than the value of the home. A final and very important consideration is whether your home is in an area where you will realize a return on your investment.

Areas of homes that are big real estate attractions are well-appointed kitchens, up-

The greatest expense in painting is the labor! Labor costs for painting can be thousands of dollars; paint costs equate to only hundreds. For a long-lasting job, select a quality product, correctly prepare the surface that is to be painted, and properly apply the paint.

to-date master baths, and large, customized master bedroom closets. Old appliances can be replaced for more attractive and efficient ones. If you have the time and money, give the considered rooms a total renovation with new floor tiles, new cabinets and fixtures, and new plumbing. You can also upgrade these rooms without doing a total renovation by repairing and repainting areas that need attention and by changing curtains (including shower/tub hangings). If you repaint areas, remember that neutral or light-colored paint makes them appear larger.

For information about licensing or building permit regulations related to home renovations, contact your local housing authority or city hall. Also, check the zoning laws and building codes before you make a major renovation. After the renovation is completed, be sure your insurance policy covers the added value of your home.

Maintain continuity! If you are adding a deck, porch, or room, the add-ons should look as though they were originally built with the home. Consider the lines, style, and materials of the existing structure when you plan your changes. Do you want to match materials exactly or find something complementary? If you have an older home, matching materials, styles, and colors may be more difficult. Exterior surfaces, such as bricks and siding, that have weathered can be hard to match. Lumber sizes change, so research the extra cost of the millwork (which can be prohibitive) before you undertake your considered outside changes.

CHOOSING A CONTRACTOR

Unless you are extremely handy, you should hire a professional contractor to complete renovations. Don't take any major investment in your home lightly. When researching contractors, compare at least

three and ask the same prepared questions of all. Don't hesitate to tell them (subtly) that you are shopping. While making comparisons is time-consuming, it is time well spent. You will find more competitive pricing as well as more ideas and options for the job. During your interview find out how long the contractor has been in business, if he is covered by liability insurance should damage occur to your property or a neighbor's, and whether the contractor and related employees are covered by workmen's compensation.

Although a deposit for contracted work is a reasonable request, don't complete payment for the job until you are completely satisfied and the contractor has done everything according to the contract. For protection you can establish an escrow account to hold your funds and have payments released in stages as the work is completed. Finalize all contracts before signing and outline all renovations, costs, and terms. If you make changes as the remodeling proceeds, these should be noted in the contract and initialed by both parties. After the renovation is completed, contact your insurance carrier to adjust your policy to include the added value to your home.

HOME SALES AND TAX IMPLICATIONS

You completed your renovations, sold your home, and have another waiting in the wings. Is it time to sit back and relax? Not quite yet. There is just one small item left to finish your move. Yes, taxes.

Certain expenditures made while moving, buying a new home, and renovating can equate to a tax deduction on your income tax. And after all those renovations you've just completed, you can probably use them. The first step is to talk to your accountant. Many of these deductions may be claimed in the current year, but some can be applied in the next year, too. A few can be spread out over a number of years.

If you are confident enough to file your own income tax, then you will need to request Form 521 (for the year in which you moved) from the Internal Revenue Service (800–829–3676). This form will outline specifics for all situations with the allowable deductions. Examples of points that make a difference in tax dollars are time of move; military, retiree, and marital status; two-income returns; self-employment; work-related moves; housing costs; and distance traveled to work. Be sure to save all your receipts for the expenses incurred.

If you found a new job and moved because of it, you may deduct miscellaneous itemized expenditures. Some possible write-offs are résumé printing costs, postage, telephone calls, interview travel costs, and employment agency fees.

If you are a recent homebuyer, you should be able to deduct all the points you

CLOSE-UP
Selling a Home on Your Own

1. Get a standard contract form from your local stationery store or a real estate firm to complete your home sale transaction. Go over all of the possible contingencies that you think a buyer might want.
2. Consider getting an appraisal of your property to help you validate your price. The appraiser may make recommendations to you for good presentation.
3. In advance, estimate what closing costs are going to be by talking to a title insurance company; find out exactly what paperwork will need to be completed, so closing will not be slowed down, interrupted, or prevented.
4. Advertise your open-house dates and hours (allow four hours). Sunday is the traditional day.
5. Be sure to include day and evening phone numbers in the ad.
6. Be prepared to commit time each weekend to open-house activities.
7. Allow visitors to tour your home at their own pace. Don't follow them through the house unless you are asked to do so.
8. When you've found a willing buyer and after the buyer has read the contract, he or she should provide you with a simple financial statement and a 5 to 10 percent "earnest money" deposit. The contract should specify how long the buyer has to get bank confirmation of loan eligibility or to take care of such contingencies as inspections. Give the buyer your disclosure forms.
9. Learn how to prequalify potential buyers by talking to mortgage bankers. They will be likely to have a basic form for buyers to complete.
10. You have the responsibility of verifying the validity of the buyer's offer and whether he or she qualifies for home buying. This means you must ensure that the buyer is able to afford the property. You must also check buyer's credit history. (The general guideline is that the buyer's monthly payment should not be more than 28 percent of the gross monthly salary. The buyer's debt ratio and credit history affect the gross salary.)

paid on your mortgage loan whether or not you paid half or none of them. If you sold a home and bought another, you can also claim some of these expenses on your income tax. Taxes and compensations change often and, depending on your circumstances (i.e., employment or distance of move), it may be more lucrative to claim these same costs as moving expenses instead of home transaction expenses. Any income reimbursement from your employer must also be claimed as income. (Many companies will automatically deduct the tax from your allowance.) For more information on the deductions and what forms to use, contact your accountant or the IRS at (800) 829–1040.

SELLING A HOME ON YOUR OWN

Selling a home on your own is definitely a task you can accomplish. Before you clap your hands thinking about the money you are going to save in commissions, you need to know what is involved. Your first priority in a home sale transaction is to obtain the necessary assistance to protect yourself, legally and financially. Current laws favor the buyer, so if you venture into sales on your own, you should have a competent real estate lawyer to guide you.

Some of the chores you need to tackle include advertising, home showings, clos-ing costs, appraisals, paperwork, and taking steps to ensure that you have a qualified homebuyer. If you require that prospective buyers be prequalified for a mortgage, it will eliminate those who house-hunt just out of curiosity and it will ensure that all individuals who respond to the advertisement are qualified buyers. *Preapproval* and *prequalifying* are explained in the Mortgages chapter.

You will save real estate commissions by selling your home without representation, but you must take precautions. We do not necessarily advocate selling a home yourself for several reasons. Your home will not be on the Multiple Listing Service; many corporate relocaters seek real estate agents who access the MLS for their clients, so you would lose that side of the market. Generally speaking, the home sale success rate for self-sellers is lower than selling with an agent. However, that is not to say that it can't be done, because some people do so, and very successfully. If you follow this path, beware of the pitfalls (such as taking your home off the market for two to three weeks only to find out that the buyer cannot qualify for a mortgage) and be sure that you take the necessary steps to protect yourself financially and legally.

REAL ESTATE AGENTS

The previous chapter outlines ways to prepare your home for a profitable sale. A significant part of this process is choosing the right real estate agent. There are many thousands of real estate agents in the United States alone, all with varying degrees of expertise. Your goal is to select someone with whom you feel comfortable, who will prepare a sensible marketing plan, and who will help you realize a sound financial transaction. There is more to being a good real estate agent than placing your home on the Multiple Listing Service!

SELECTING A REAL ESTATE AGENT

One way to begin your search for the right person to represent you in a home sale is by asking a colleague or friend for a recommendation, preferably someone who has previously used the real estate agent's services. You want an agent who is familiar with home sales in your price range and in your neighborhood. It is important to feel comfortable with the agent during an interview because comfort level and good communications are critical.

To help you choose a knowledgeable and qualified real estate agent, inquire about client references (ask for two or three and qualify these), the agent's credentials, licensing, and area of real estate expertise, how well the agent knows the community you are considering, and the types of homes he or she typically sells. It is also reasonable to ask about the number of homes the agent has listed and actually sold, and how recently those sales took place. Longevity is not necessarily the best yardstick for a real estate agent. You need someone who is pursuing sales, returning telephone calls, and aggressively working in your best interest. Compare each agent's commission fees as well, because fees can be negotiable depending on the market and current competition.

Remember, the agent you choose is going to be your main source of information and should advise and guide you in many ways. If you don't get the responses you desire during an interview, there are lots of agencies to choose from. The selection process can take time, but the end result will be well worth it and will put money in your pocket.

AGENT'S MARKETING PLANS

Find out what your agent proposes as a plan to sell your property. At the very minimum a real estate agent should suggest

HomeFair.com (www.homefair.com) offers information about real estate agents, schools, salaries, communities, a moving calculator, rent-versus-buying calculator, how to find a mover or a builder, senior community living, and much more.

newspaper ads and direct mail to advertise your home. Ask about other advertising specifics and formats, such as brochures and flyers. You also want to know the timing of your promotion—when, where, and how long the advertisements will run. Other beneficial marketing efforts are weekend open houses and promoting your home to other agents in the area. You need to know what marketing efforts you can expect from your prospective agent so that you're not left with some vague idea of what he or she will do for you. Request to receive the marketing plan in writing with the option to revise it if the plan is not working.

HOME WARRANTIES

Consider purchasing a home warranty, which is a relatively small investment in this huge transaction and can increase the potential for a satisfactory sale. Warranties are an important sales tool, especially if the resale market is slow. Typically, sellers purchase half of all warranties, but they can also opt to pay the entire cost, making the transaction more attractive. Wouldn't you be happier if someone told you the home you are buying has a home warranty that will cover your major appliances and heating and air-conditioning units for one full year?

Don't substitute a warranty for a home inspection, but consider it as peace of mind for both you and the buyer. When you purchase a warranty plan, be selective and examine the fine print. There are often

Reports about your home's activity from your real estate agent should be on Mondays because weekends present the most opportunities for viewing and open houses.

several deductibles, and some warranties are more inclusive than others.

OFFERS AND COUNTEROFFERS

When you get to the point of receiving an actual offer for your home, you can either accept it as it is or you can counteroffer. To decide how you will proceed, you will have to assess your finances, the housing market, and your current circumstances.

When you receive an offer that does not meet your asking price, you may consider accepting it under these circumstances: You need the money for another home; it's the first offer in over one month; it's a buyer's market right now; or you will realize enough money to recoup some or most of your investment.

When do you consider making a counteroffer? You should consider a counteroffer when the following apply: The offer is unreasonably low (compared with appropriate and/or recent home sales in your area); buyers are plentiful in your area; or you're in a position to risk losing your prospect entirely. If you decide to counteroffer, reduce your asking price in relatively small increments.

If you do not wish to counteroffer, you would be wise to substantiate your quoted price with evidence that makes your case. For example, perhaps you bought brandnew carpeting, have had your entire downstairs repainted, or installed a new heating system. An appraisal also can help you to validate your price.

Some buyers will dismiss a house altogether if their initial offer is not accepted. This may simply be because they can't afford it, they may have another house in mind, or they may be just scouting homes. Real estate agents say that relatively few buyers want to actively negotiate a home transaction.

ARM YOUR AGENT

Your agent needs to know as much as possible about your home and the features that set it apart from the competition to do a competent job for you. It will help to sell your home quickly if the agent can easily justify the cost of your home to prospective clients. Think carefully about everything in your home that makes a difference to you. Be sure to include the new heating/AC unit, heavy-duty appliances, or an extensive alarm system. Remember all the additional assets, such as extra telephone lines, multiple television outlets, lighting features, large closets, and extra thick carpeting. The comforts that you appreciate will most likely be valued by the potential

Most counties will allow you to research the current deed transactions for little or no cost. The best way to get a feel for the market is to research similar homes in your area and their selling prices.

buyer as well. Gather facts such as average utility costs, annual property taxes, maintenance records, a list of repairs and/or renovations, and any other attributes that set your home apart from others in the area. Finally, your home should be in picture-perfect condition for each and every showing. You and your family (and pets) should vacate the home during all open houses.

MORTGAGES

Before you begin mortgage shopping, take time to review all of your assets and liabilities and then calculate your present financial situation. Be sure to detail your ability to pay whatever debts you currently have. Mortgage lenders say that lightening your credit load and terminating unused credit cards are two of the best ways to improve your credit rating.

Next, look for a lender. You want to select someone who you believe is really listening to you. A knowledgeable financier should be able to evaluate your financial position and arrange the best loan plan for your circumstances.

Variables that can make a difference when qualifying for a mortgage are the amount of equity you have for a down payment, your employment and job stability, your debt ratio/fixed debt amount, and your gross income. Many mortgage options are available today, and you can begin by doing some research on the Internet (input "mortgage" in the search field), where you will find new information almost weekly regarding types of mortgages and special offers. The most important part about mortgage shopping is to take the time to educate yourself. Don't simply depend on the advice of a friend. Some mortgage guidelines are outlined in this chapter, but it is up to you to compare lenders and services, as well as to ask questions to understand your options.

COMPARISON SHOPPING

If you're new at the mortgage game, you may not realize how substantially different deals and fees can be from lender to lender. So shop around. A few percentage points here and there can definitely affect your monthly payments. Compare loan rates using information from local banks, mortgage companies, the newspaper, and the local Board of Realtors. Include costs in your comparisons, which typically include legal fees, appraisal fees, title insurance fees, prepayment penalties, and points. All fees affect your estimates and the quoted interest rate. As of January 1993, full disclosure of all brokerage fees and lenders' compensation was federally mandated. If you are making a work-related move, ask your relocation manager if the company deals with a lender who will offer you preferred financing, and what, if any, financial assistance you can expect.

Carefully consider your finances. Calculate whether you will have enough money on which to live after paying the expenses associated with a mortgage. Be sure that you understand the additional costs that are involved in closing on a house. These usually include the attorney's fees, application fee and points, appraisal fee, property survey, home inspection, credit report, title search and insurance, mortgage and homeowner's insurance, and fees for document preparation and notary services.

Many aspects in mortgage lending are negotiable. Ask the lender what he or she is going to do for you. You need to know how the lender can help you achieve the right mortgage package and to be assured that your business is important to the lending institution.

If you are a first-time homebuyer or are unfamiliar with all the terminology of a mortgage contract, request legal advice before you sign the contract after assuring that all costs that you agreed upon are detailed on this form. Any agreement that you sign regarding "earnest money" should have a clause to refund all of your money if the deal doesn't go through.

PREQUALIFYING AND PREAPPROVAL

Obtaining preapproval for a mortgage before your house-hunting trip is a smart way to avoid lost time, money, and frustration. Don't underestimate this step. Some real estate agents and buyer brokers actually require that their clients be preapproved prior to home shopping because it shows buyers are serious shoppers and it expedites sales. If you shop for a mortgage before you look at homes, you will have a more realistic idea of what mortgages and terms are available and the amount of money for which you qualify. The exercise of prequalifying improves your bargaining power with sellers; it also helps you gain some insight into credit trouble spots. If a large balance on a credit card prompts a red flag, the loan officer will advise you to reduce the debt to help you to qualify.

Loan prequalification is a fairly informal process. The lender will check credit and employment history and verify down-payment funds for a very modest fee.

After discussing the prospective buyer's financial status, the lender writes a letter (often a form letter) stating that based on the information presented to him or her, the buyer is prequalified.

Preapproval can be the next step that follows prequalification. This approval allows you assured financing for a certain dollar amount on an appropriate property. Preapprovals are relatively inexpensive and can be procured even long distance via a fax machine or using regular mail service.

Everyone's financial situation is different. Shopping around enables you to find the lender and the best mortgage for your particular financial circumstances. Loan companies can change hands (sometimes often), so inquire about the stability of your lender and how you will know of any such change.

BUYING WITHOUT A DOWN PAYMENT

If you absolutely do not have cash for a down payment on a mortgage, there are several options for you to consider. A lease option can be beneficial for the buyer and the seller. In this case, the buyer agrees to lease the seller's house for a period of time, paying a fair rent with an option to buy. All, or part of, the rent paid to date is applied to the down payment. Another option is "sweat equity." This allows the potential buyers to live in a home while they finish the necessary work on the house, crediting the value toward the down payment. A third option is using tangible assets. This involves trading a boat, car, jewelry, or valuables as a down payment on a dwelling. For lenders to approve this type of transaction, an appraisal of the item is required. If you pursue any of these options, be sure and have all the details outlined in writing.

INSURANCE, FINANCE, AND ESTATE GUIDELINES

Comprehensive and updated insurance coverage makes very good sense whether you are moving or not. However, a relocation situation is the perfect opportunity to critically evaluate your personal property or homeowner's insurance policy and update the coverage as necessary. If you have married, have had a child (or two), have changed employers, have deleted a dependent, or have been divorced, then your policy will require revisions. When it comes time to pack and ship your household goods, you want to be sure there is adequate insurance coverage in case of loss or irreparable damage during the move.

HOUSEHOLD INSURANCE

The first step is to prepare a comprehensive household inventory. An inventory should routinely be revised and updated. You can document your possessions on paper, on your computer, and/or by camera. Copy the inventory (both written lists and pictures or videos) and the insurance policy. Pack these copies among the belongings you will carry with you when you move. Store the originals in a safe-deposit box or give them to someone you trust.

To update your policy, your insurance agent will need an estimate of your household goods and valuables based on your inventory. An estimate will allow your agent

to review the coverage your homeowner's policy provides and add a "floater" if necessary for your move. If damage results during the move, the claim may be settled on a depreciated or full replacement value basis (you choose when you purchase the insurance). Remember to inform your insurance agent of your new address and relocation dates. Depreciated insurance indicates that the reimbursement given will be determined by the current value of the item, or what the item would sell for now. This amount includes consideration for age, usage, and condition (a television purchased five years ago for $350 may only be worth $50 now due to technological advancement, amount of usage, and condition).

Full replacement value insurance allows the insured to receive reimbursement equal to a brand-new, comparable item. There is no consideration given to the age or condition of the original. (A $450 television could replace the $350 model, as long as it was of similar make and contained similar features.) If your policy requires a deductible, the designated amount will be automatically deducted before reimbursement.

Do not ship flammable or otherwise hazardous materials with your household goods.

MOVING COMPANY INSURANCE

All moving companies are required to assume liability for the household goods that they transport; however, there are different levels of liability. You as a consumer should fully understand the limit of the mover's liability before the mover performs its services.

With domestic liability insurance, which is actually referred to as "valuation," all movers provide some type of minimum liability coverage. Transferees have several options in terms of insuring their household goods shipments. Generally, most corporate customers authorize movers to provide what is called full replacement value protection liability insurance. However, total liability for shipments varies, depending upon the type of liability insurance that the shipper chooses, the corporate policy, and possibly your position in the company.

Many van lines have customers complete a form that outlines customer responsibilities. For example, the form may acknowledge that if a customer wishes for the van line to transport such valuable items as jewelry, coins, currency, important documents, or collectibles, the customer must notify the van line.

Understand the moving company's rules for boxes packed by owner (referred to as "PBO"). The guidelines that usually apply are as follows: If the boxes that you pack arrive dented and damaged, you can submit a claim for broken goods within that box, but if the boxes that you pack arrive without obvious damages or dents, broken items in the box are usually your responsibility.

Additional insurance coverage may also be purchased from your insurance agent through a "floater" policy on your homeowner's or renter's insurance. The household inventory discussed in the Organizing Your Move chapter can help you to assess what your household goods are worth so that you can obtain comprehensive insurance coverage for them.

Many consumers are not aware that automobiles shipped by movers are valued at the current "blue book" value. This is the retail value for an automobile determined by the National Automobile Dealers Association based on used car sales. The only items that should be in the car when it is transported are a spare tire and the tire jack. You should not store your personal belongings in the trunk of the car before it is transported because of the risk to the car or to the contents themselves.

RENTER'S INSURANCE

If you are renting a dwelling, your landlord's insurance will not cover any of your personal property. You need to obtain renter's insurance for such items as clothing, stereo equipment, televisions and video recorders, computers, furniture, and valuables. Renter's insurance protects you from unpredictable losses due to fire or smoke, vandalism or theft, and storms. It also allows coverage in case a guest is injured in your residence. The same variables for household insurance (depreciated and full replacement value) are applicable with renter's insurance.

Shop around for renter's policies and ask about the coverage and the company's stipulations. Policies typically vary by fees, types of coverage, discounts, claim policies, special conditions, liabilities, proof of loss, theft limit, and deductibles.

If your present bank has branches in the city to which you are moving, you can have your funds electronically transferred to a new branch of your choice.

TRANSFERRING BANKING SERVICES

Among the most important details you need to attend to when you move is transferring your banking services. You want to ensure a smooth transition of accounts and services from your present bank to a suitable bank in your new community.

Before you leave your present city, take the time to visit the bank where you usually do business and meet with the bank manager or a sales representative and request that he or she send a letter of recommendation confirming your good bank standing to the prospective bank. This effort will help you avoid lengthy credit processing when you establish an account at another bank. Your employer is another source for a letter of recommendation. Ask your current supervisor to send a letter verifying your employment status with your company to the bank as well.

When you research banks in the new community, consider the convenience of their locations, the charges for their services, and the dividends they offer. You may assume the banking services that you presently have are standard, but in fact banking services can vary quite a bit. You have to think about all the services that you now enjoy, such as an automatic deposit setup for accounts, the hours of operation, and convenient ATM machines.

When researching banks, you can check into whether their ATM/debit cards are widely accepted and the national service that they are affiliated with. Ask about ATM fees and ATM withdrawal limits. You can also ask if they provide free checking, interest checking, or have free safe-deposit boxes. Does the new bank offer credit cards and overdraft protection? Does it offer savings bonds, mortgages, and brokerage services such as stock purchases, mutual funds, CDs (certificates of deposit), and IRAs (individual retirement accounts)?

With the growth of the banking industry, many banks now offer customers free services that just a few years ago came with fees. Some banks are also trying to make services more convenient and have set up twenty-four-hour toll-free numbers. Many banks are accessible through the Internet and allow you to write and send checks electronically. ATM machines are offering more and more services besides just dispensing cash. These services allow customers to check balances, transfer funds, and do many other transactions quickly without actually going to the bank.

Be sure you are fully established in a bank of your choice before you terminate your former accounts. You will need to close out your safe-deposit box and savings and checking accounts, pay off your mortgage and loans, and leave a forwarding address with a bank representative.

ESTATE PLANNING

The primary goals of estate planning are to establish how you want to leave your estate and how to make sure your beneficiaries don't pay high taxes on it. Anyone over the age of 21 should have a will, preferably one that has been written by a lawyer. The size of your estate will dictate how detailed and complex your will becomes. Then there are living wills, powers-of-attorney, trust funds, and life insurance policies, to name a few. All of these should be updated if you recently moved to a new state or if you now have residences in several states. It is very important to establish where your domicile is. Therefore, the documents need to be discussed with both your lawyer and accountant so that your heirs are not fighting in court for years to come.

Nearly every state has a law stating that if a will is valid in the jurisdiction in which it was signed, it will be valid in the new state of domicile. Other estate planning documents such as advance health care directives or powers-of-attorney will also generally be given effect in another state. Therefore, there is no need to see a lawyer or financial planner immediately before or after you move, but it is advisable to review your estate plan and update it within a year or so after you relocate.

If you move from one state to another and you intend to permanently reside in the new state, it is important that you clearly establish your new domicile. If you die and it is unclear where your domicile was, both (or several) states may claim your domicile is in their jurisdiction and attempt to collect death taxes.

A few ways to establish your domicile are registering to vote, applying for a new driver's license, and establishing state and local income tax returns for the new jurisdiction. The next step is to take your existing estate planning documents to an attorney in the new jurisdiction to review and update them. This includes living wills or advance health care declarations, durable powers-of-attorney, and your will and/or trust. Your revised estate plan should take into account any special provisions of your new state's laws.

To locate a new attorney when you move, a referral from a trusted attorney is advisable. You can also ask neighbors, colleagues, or associates for a recommendation. Inquire about a prospective attorney's fees and services and compare them with your previous legal assistance.

If you move out of the country for any period of time (and particularly if you acquire property in other countries), special considerations apply, and your estate planner will have to assist you in this regard. Likewise, if either you or your spouse is not a United States citizen, special estate planning rules apply and require your attention.

i *If you need some ready cash and your home is completely paid for, consider obtaining a reverse mortgage. This arrangement allows a buyer who owns mortgage-free property to obtain income. The lender makes monthly payments to the borrower, using the property as collateral. Be sure to read the fine print about any mortgage agreement and understand all the service fees, interest rates, and the payment schedule, and make sure you talk to your lawyer and accountant before you sign on the dotted line.*

MOVING COMPANIES

If you are making a corporate move, your employer most likely has one or several moving companies that it typically uses for its employees. If you are moving without the benefit of corporate assistance, select and compare three well-known or recommended companies. Your comparison should include prices, services, and policies. Ask the company representative for company literature, moving tips, a free estimate, and references of satisfied clients. Call these clients and ask them about the company's professionalism, dependability, and attention to detail before, during, and after the move.

Your selection should also depend on the length of time the company is in business; the care taken when moving; the costs for packing, mileage, and unloading; insurance, liability, discounts, and tracking methods for your goods in transit; and the company's on-time record and safe and dry storage facilities. This last point is very important because you don't want to find out a year after your move that your belongings (that you thought were safely stored) are instead mildewed and damaged beyond repair. Take your time in this process because you will be entrusting all your worldly possessions to the company that you choose.

CONTRACTS

After you have selected a company and a moving date, your moving company representative will prepare a contract for you.

Before you sign any contract, be sure everything that you have verbally agreed upon is typed into the fine print. The contract should specify the number of hours for your move and all the charges and terms.

For your representative to give you a proper cost estimate, he or she needs to know everything that will be involved in your move, including what will be transported, such as the number of rooms of furniture, special furniture requirements, and any extras that will be moved (such as an automobile). In addition, the moving company needs the accessibility details about both your old and new homes. It should be made aware if there are three levels of steps at one of the residences, if one of the driveways is especially steep, the house is a long distance from the road, or whether there are any other particulars that will hamper or delay the moving process.

ESTIMATES

Moving companies typically offer two kinds of estimates: binding and nonbinding. A binding estimate ensures that the price quoted for your move is a firm price for the agreed-upon services, so that there are no unexpected charges at the completion of the move. This estimate must be in writing and a copy should be attached to the bill of lading. You can be charged for this estimate.

A nonbinding estimate means you will not know the final charges until the movers establish actual weights and transportation charges. The mover cannot charge for this estimate. If you are given a nonbinding estimate, the mover will require payment of the original estimate at the time of delivery.

WEIGHTS AND PAYMENTS

Movers are supposed to weigh the truck when it is empty and again when they load your household goods. If there is a discrepancy between the departure and destination weights, you can request that the truck be reweighed.

Payment of moves (unless you made prior arrangements) is typically by money order or certified check. Payment may be expected upon delivery of your goods, prior to unloading. If you have agreed to pay charges at delivery, obtain the weight and charges before the movers unload the truck.

Local move charges are gauged by hours involved for packing goods, types and number of cartons used, and the time involved to handle your shipment. Interstate moves depend more on the weight of the household goods and the distance of transportation. Corporate moves usually have an estimate that includes all moving costs.

If you are moving from October to April, there is less demand for a mover's services; therefore, costs may be lower and more negotiable. It may also be easier to obtain your first choice for a moving date. Note that scheduling can be difficult during the Christmas and New Year holidays because of vacations and holiday leaves.

---

i *If you expect to move during the peak moving season (May to September), schedule your move months in advance, and then a few weeks prior to the date, call and confirm the arrangements and the schedule.*

RIGHTS AND RESPONSIBILITIES

If you are making a long-distance move, know and understand the moving company's procedures and necessary agent contacts. Be sure the destination agent has your telephone number or a contact in the new area. You also need to have the phone number and name of the destination agent. When you plan your move, allow a few extra days in your schedule. There can be unforeseen problems that can cause delays, such as inclement weather, a mechanical problem with the moving van, a personal problem, or traffic and/or construction delays encountered en route.

Pick-up and delivery dates should be as specific as possible—between 8:00 and 9:00 A.M. is good; "sometime in the morning" is not. When you and the mover have agreed on these terms, the mover must abide by the schedule or notify you of a problem causing a delay. In the event of a problem, the mover should reschedule a time that is convenient for you.

Before finalizing a move, inquire about the mover's policy for inconvenience claims. If the company does not pick up or deliver within the promised time and it is clearly at fault, it should reimburse you for out-of-pocket expenses, such as lodging and meals.

THE MOVING PROCESS

First, a sales representative will contact you. This is your contact person within the moving company. The representative will tour your home with you, and he or she will note the estimated weight of your goods and any unusual requirements. Be prepared for this visit by listing items that require special attention or services you want (such as transferring large houseplants, antiques, or valuables). Ask questions, get a business card, and request to have all details included in the contract.

The representative will arrange the pick-up, delivery, and storage dates.

Next, you will meet the packers. Walk through your home with the packers, orienting them with the rooms and your belongings that require special care. Point out the goods that are not to be packed. Before the packers leave, the supervisor will give you forms, which itemize each carton. You will need to sign them and then pass them on to the driver.

On moving out day your household goods will be organized and loaded onto the truck. All your belongings will be detailed on the packing forms and damaged or marked areas (on the furniture) will be noted. After your goods are completely loaded, you will need to review all paperwork. Moving companies use codes to denote types of marks or damage, and the key to these codes should be on the form. Make sure you agree, because these codes are used to dispute claims you may file upon delivery. A slight chip should not be marked as "broken."

On moving in day, you or a reliable friend will need to be at your new residence at the agreed-upon time of delivery for your goods. If no one is at your residence at this time, the mover can reschedule the move at its convenience or put your goods in storage at your expense. Have a moving form handy and designate someone to examine the furniture and check off the goods on the form as the movers come through the door. This effort will ensure that you have all of your household goods. If you move in February and find in November that an antique turkey platter is missing, it may be too late to make a claim.

Any good move is a cooperative effort between you and the mover. Begin your moving day by making introductions and use the movers' names when addressing them; it is important to establish this pro-

fessional relationship for the day(s) the movers will be in your home. Take the time to show them around your home, pointing out special requests. Any special instructions should be well marked and mentioned to the movers.

To expedite the moving process, use the room plans discussed in the Organizing Your Move chapter. If you have an extra person, he or she can begin unpacking boxes (especially if the movers are willing to remove the cartons). Begin by unpacking the larger boxes, such as clothing boxes, and items that belong in kitchen cabinets. The movers can take many of the larger boxes with them, and it will be convenient to have your kitchen in operating condition as soon as possible (unless of course you want to extend your trips to restaurants).

It is a nice gesture to have nonalcoholic beverages available, and, although it is not required, we always purchased take-out meals for our movers. Many companies have policies of nonacceptance of gratuities, which can include meals; therefore, asks the sales representative about the policy. It is also nice to have soap and paper towels available. Let the movers know where to find these necessities so they can help themselves to everything.

If you have any unusual problems on moving day, speak to the driver, who is usually the person in charge at the site. If the issue is not resolved, you can contact the company sales representative.

Try to remain calm. Movers are used to customers feeling harried and will try to help you feel confident that things will work out well. Remember, you are a customer and this is your home with your personal property and you should expect professional courtesy, while recognizing that the movers have a huge job to do with your best interest at heart.

MOVING ON YOUR OWN

If you are planning to rent a truck and move yourself, you should begin organizing as soon as you make the decision to move. You will need time to evaluate truck rental companies, collect your materials, wrap and pack your household goods, and engage dependable help for the loading and unloading of your goods. If possible, ask friends who have been through a moving experience themselves to assist you in this final step.

CHOOSING A TRUCK RENTAL COMPANY

You will need to make a reservation to rent a truck at least one month before you plan to move, and earlier if you are moving during peak (May to September) moving time. Before you rent a truck, however, you need to evaluate the companies. You want to be sure you have a company with which you are satisfied and that offers the truck size that you will need. Call three companies and compare services, discounts, mileage costs, and convenience of contacts (in case of unexpected problems on the road). Don't hesitate to ask the representative about the age of the company's trucks and the maintenance records of its vehicles. Review each company's policies for insurance and liability so that you, your helpers, and your household effects will be adequately insured. Also check on your own policy because some policies cover rental trucks.

An updated household inventory is necessary so that you can place a comprehensive and up-to-date valuation on your goods. This inventory will help if you have an insurance claim, and knowing the quantity of goods will help you to estimate the truck size that you will need. The rental company can suggest the best truck size for you if you tell the representative the number of furnished rooms that you have to move. At this time, you can also reserve other equipment, such as furniture ties, dollies, hand trucks (for heavy appliances), blankets, and pads. After you have compared companies, pick one and reserve the truck you need. Everything that you discussed with the company representative should be outlined in writing; review your contract.

PACKING AND MATERIALS

Collect as much packing material as possible and as early as possible. As soon as you know you are moving, begin saving bubble wrap, tissue paper, and styrofoam packing from shipments you receive at your home. Purchase cording or rope to secure the furniture in the truck. You will need enough rope to tie down your furniture about every one-quarter of the truck capacity to minimize movement during transportation.

Wrapping paper can be purchased from moving or truck rental companies as well as office supply stores. Newspaper is

Do not allow electronic equipment, especially computers, to be in extremely hot or cold temperatures for any length of time.

good for padding the bottoms of boxes, but do not use it for wrapping because the ink will rub off on your belongings. Stock up on package-sealing tape, marking pens, and labels. Save or collect sturdy boxes, such as liquor store and bookstore boxes. Used boxes also can be purchased from moving or truck rental companies. Consider purchasing the large wardrobe boxes. These boxes are especially strong, transport clothing well, and the bottom of the box can be utilized for sweaters and reasonably lightweight unbreakables. Moving and truck rental companies also sell mattress boxes, book boxes, and kitchen barrel boxes.

Remember, you will have to do all the wrapping and packing yourself, so you may want to pack in stages. You can begin with seasonal items, such as Christmas ornaments if you are moving in May. Be sure to mark all breakables carefully. If you use colored paper for tiny objects there is less chance of losing them in the mountain of paper. Wrap, pad, and pack pictures and mirrors in cardboard containers. Use every nook and cranny of space to place items: You can pack light, unbreakable items inside of appliances such as a refrigerator, washer, or dryer. (Remember to unpack these same appliances before use!) You can also pack small pictures in drawers that are not completely filled, padding the items with towels or sweaters.

If you are moving out of state, find out if you can transport your houseplants into the state before you worry about packing them. If you cannot take your plants along, or if you choose not to move them, consider donating them to a charitable organization or a home for the elderly.

If you plan to take your plants with you, they should be among the last items to be packed. Water plants sparingly and allow them to drain (overnight if possible) while you are packing everything else. A method we used to transport plants was to place them inside portable shelving. The shelving can be packed at the rear of the truck standing sideways, with the plants placed inside the openings. You have to decide if the plant is worth the effort and expense of moving it. Plants also make nice good-bye gifts to your neighbors and friends.

APPLIANCE PREPARATION

Check all the appliance manuals for directions about how to prepare appliances for moving. Washers, dryers, and refrigerators require special care. The refrigerator needs to be cleaned and defrosted, the oven and range require cleaning, and the washing machine should be properly drained and prepared as well. Casters on refrigerators and freezers have to be recessed, or the units have to be secured in the truck so they do not move during your transition. Motors and compressors on some appliances should be secured before they are transported. You can contact a professional appliance service company if you are not sure how to prepare your appliances for a move, if the appliances were professionally installed, or if you do not have the proper equipment. If you engage service technicians, ask them to explain the procedure to set up these same appliances at your destination or arrange for professional services at your new residence.

Details for appliance care should be in the owner's manuals. Dry the interiors of all your appliances. Remove fittings and accessories, pack them in a small plastic bag, and place them inside of the appliance. Tightly secure all the doors, hoses, and cords with rope or tape.

STEREO EQUIPMENT, RADIOS, AND COMPUTERS

Computers, stereo equipment, radios, clocks, toasters, and small appliances should be packed according to the directions in the owner's manuals and preferably packaged in their original cartons. If you no longer have these containers, pack them in boxes with styrofoam "popcorn" packing material and clearly label each box. They should be marked with the type of equipment, the name of the item, and when applicable, EXTREMELY FRAGILE in bold letters. Clearly mark all wires for electronic equipment and pack them with the appliance.

Computers take some extra care. All of the cords that are attached to your movable hardware (such as a mouse) should be disconnected and labeled. "Park" your PC by inserting a blank floppy into the disk drive. All equipment should be detached, but keep the cords with each piece. Don't forget to back up all your hard drive files onto a floppy disk and keep them in your possession en route to your new residence.

If you have any questions about moving your computer or electronics, consult the manuals that came with the equipment for packing and transportation instructions. You can make any additional inquiries at your local computer store.

ORGANIZING YOUR HELP

Be sure you stress to your "volunteers" that work needs to begin as soon as the truck arrives at your home. Ask them to be available to assist you during the entire loading process. It is very important that you start on time in order to avoid costly delays. A two-hour delay could ultimately cost you an extra day's rental fee for the truck and equipment.

When your helpers arrive, take them on a tour of your home, reviewing the household items that need to be packed and the loading procedure that you wish to follow. Ask them for suggestions and be sure everyone has a clear understanding of what needs to be accomplished and your scheduled time frame.

Tell the helpers that there will be coffee and doughnuts when they arrive and that lunch and cold drinks and water will be provided throughout the day. Have ice and a cooler available. Don't serve alcoholic beverages—it will slow the job down and be dangerous as well. Instead, buy your helpers a gift certificate to their favorite restaurant as a thank-you.

LOADING THE TRUCK

Begin by loading the heavier furniture and appliances at the cab (the front) of the truck. Pack everything as tightly as possible. Tie strong rope around the furniture from one side of the truck to the other. Your goods will move somewhat in the truck as you travel no matter how tightly you pack them, so the extra security of the rope is very important. Load pictures and mirrors on the truck sideways in order to prevent breakage, and if possible pack them in between mattresses and the box springs. Some trucks have a special section for fragile items. Heavy boxes of equal weight can be packed one on top of the other.

Truck sizes vary, but all major self-help companies agree on the approximate number of rooms that can fit into each size van. A 10-foot van can hold furniture from one to two rooms. A 14- to 15-foot van can handle two to three rooms. An 18- to 20-foot van is big enough for four to five rooms, and a 22- to 24-foot van can hold furniture from six to eight rooms.

Keep the toolbox handy in case you have to remove doors or disassemble furniture. The toolbox should also be packed last in the truck so it is accessible for road emergencies and for necessities at your new location.

TRAVEL PLANNING

You cannot travel in a truck as fast as you can in an automobile. Plan to travel no more than 300 miles a day when driving a large self-move truck. Take a travel companion with you who can help with the unloading, and allow at least one day in your schedule to remove everything from the truck. If you do not have someone who can make the trip, be sure to arrange for help at your destination. You can ask your employer, a colleague, or a neighbor in the new area for suggestions. Don't forget to pencil meals, lodging, gas, and tolls (which may be higher with a truck than a car) into your budget.

Be sure you know the telephone numbers and procedures to obtain service and assistance for your rental truck on your travel route in case a problem should arise. The last thing you need (now that you have completed all the packing, cleaning, and loading) is to have a mechanical breakdown or a flat tire during your trip to your new home. AAA members can get trip-planning help from that organization; make sure to tell the AAA representative that you are driving a moving van so he or she can plan your route accordingly and book you in motels with discounts. Note the height of the truck; depending on the truck's size, you might be forced to use truck stops for fuel if the truck does not fit under the canopies of regular gas stations.

Each time you stop, you should walk around the truck and inspect the tires, lights, and doors. If you stop for the night or longer, secure the truck with a sturdy padlock and park in a well-lighted or visible area. If you have a connection or are pulling a trailer, these should be checked and locked as well.

A PRE-MOVE VISIT TO THE NEW COMMUNITY

Before you load the moving van, you have to know where you are going. That means you need to do advance scouting of your destination. This "pre-move" process involves everything from getting a good idea about your prospective new community to finding a place to live in the new town.

If you are moving because of your job, most companies reimburse employees for at least one pre-move visit to find a home and survey the community. If your move is a personal choice, you will need to plan a visit at your own expense. With the varying cultures throughout the United States, any move has the potential to require many changes in your life. These can include basics such as everyday attire, names of products, accepted behaviors, food, and entertainment, all of which equate to a type of culture shock that affects people more than they expect. With these thoughts in mind, you will realize that the costs that are incurred for this type of visit will be repaid many times over after you move.

PREPARING FOR THE VISIT

Before you set off on your pre-move visit, make a list of resources to check, considering everything that is important to your family. Your most important goal during this visit is to find, and hopefully purchase, a new home. Homes you consider should have a good proximity to schools, work,

place of worship, and anything else that your family will require, such as day care or elder care.

When surveying housing, think about what you have previously enjoyed in the way of living arrangements. For instance, do you like being able to walk from your home to the grocery store? Or perhaps you enjoy the peace and quiet of country life. Save a few days of your trip to learn about the area because this may be your only chance to become familiar with it before you move. While house-hunting, note room sizes, particularly the family room, bedrooms, and kitchen. See the Organizing Your Move chapter for tips on measuring the furniture and factoring room sizes.

Acquire a city map and pick up a local telephone directory, which will help you accomplish many tasks from a distance after you return home. Visit the chamber of commerce to learn about activities and functions in the city and try to locate services that are important to your family. You especially want to locate doctors' and dentists' offices, pharmacies, the nearest hospital, shopping areas, and facilities such as

---

Know the closest facility to obtain routine and emergency medical care. Moving places added stress on people and accidents and illness are more likely to occur before, during, or after a move.

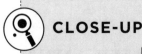

CLOSE-UP

Education Resources

The following resources can help you with information on schools and day care centers:

Private Independent Schools is a comprehensive annual guide to elementary and secondary schools in North America and abroad. It includes objective and easy-to-read articles on the schools and information on counseling services helpful to relocating families. Contact Private Independent Schools at 238 North Main Street, Wallingford, CT 06492, call (203) 269–3333, or visit the Web site www.buntingand lyon.com.

Child Care Aware operates a national toll-free information line (800–424–2246) and Web site (www.childcareaware.org) that provides child care information and other parenting resources to families in both English and Spanish. Child Care Aware connects families to local child care experts, including resource and referral centers, that assist families in finding, selecting, and paying for child care and other parenting needs. Child Care Aware is funded through a cooperative agreement with the Child Care Bureau of the U.S. Department of Health and Human Services.

You can also input your new city's name and "school" into any Internet search engine to review the schools in the new community.

churches, restaurants, and dry cleaners—basically anything that your family will require on a routine basis. If time permits, stop in to the various agencies or centers you are evaluating to introduce yourself. Be sure to pick up business cards in order to keep the names, services, and their locations on file for when you return. It is becoming more common for companies to assist relocating employees with these types of services, so be sure to ask your company relocation manager if relocation assistance is available.

Visit several banks to evaluate their services, and then open an account at the institution you have chosen, one that is convenient to your home and daily activities. If you open an account and reserve a safe-deposit box on this trip, you will be able to cash checks for local services much

more easily. It will also eliminate the expense of wiring funds to a new bank as you are moving and the charges to use an ATM machine.

SCHOOL GUIDE

Include school shopping in this trip so you can evaluate a school and its faculty in person. Visiting the school will assist you in forming an opinion of its environment, values, and capabilities, as well as the personalities and skills of the teachers. During your visit discuss any special requirements that your children have and review their school records and transcripts, course descriptions, and describe their previous school programs with the staff.

Selecting the right school begins with making sure the courses correlate with students' last school and their aspirations for further education. If a prospective school is very dissimilar to your children's previous schools, ask yourself if and how they will benefit from attending this particular school. Inquire at the local library or the state or county departments of education for schools' standardized test results and post-graduation placements in colleges, armed forces, and other institutions, such as art academies. The right school will make all the difference to you and your children, so take your time in this process and follow your instincts.

DAY CARE CENTERS

After you obtain recommendations and information about at least three centers, visit each site and speak with the instructors so you can form an opinion of each center's environment, cleanliness, values, and capabilities. Keep in mind that the most important things to youngsters aren't computers, flashy toys, or dramatic surroundings. What matters is each child's experience.

When choosing a center make sure it has the following:

- State licensing and accreditation.
- A small pupil-to-teacher ratio.
- Teachers with training in early childhood education.

If you will be living in temporary quarters, you can sign a form at the post office near your new home and arrange to have your mail held at the station. This will mean more trips to the post office, but it is far easier than changing your address twice.

- A bright and cheery environment that provides creative daily activities, a well-planned schedule, and outdoor playtime.
- Compliance with fire and building safety codes.
- Children who are happily occupied and seem to easily approach their caregiver when they need help or attention.

After your visit is over, schedule a moving date so you can make arrangements for utility and other relevant services to begin at your new home before you move in. Then, follow up upon your arrival to be sure all services have been established. Accomplishing the above items on your pre-move visit is ideal; however, you may not have the time to do everything. If not, be sure to do so as soon as possible after you arrive in the new city.

HOW TO BE A SAVVY HOME BUYER

Purchasing a home is one of the biggest financial decisions most people make in their lifetime. Before you take the plunge to become a homeowner, be sure you take stock of your cash flow and your available funds. You need to consider that as a homeowner you will be responsible not only for the purchase price but also for the maintenance, repair, and upgrading of a residence. All too often people unknowingly become "house poor" due to home purchase obligations and experience a less than satisfactory existence that does not meet their expectation.

Determine at the outset what you need (and can afford) and what you would like to have in a home. Your real estate representative needs to understand your daily needs and lifestyle. For instance, your agent should be aware of your children's grade levels and expectations for education, the family's interests and activities, transportation requirements (including whether you require frequent air travel), whether a home office is important, your work locations, a realistic mortgage budget, and, last but not least, when your next move could take place.

Buying is an emotional process. We buy something because we desire it. And home purchases certainly fall into this category. So don't let your emotional attachment preclude your rational judgment as you shop for a home.

Gather information on a house in your price range and desired location. Talk to people who already live in the neighborhood, asking about the safety, children's play activities, and adult camaraderie. If you receive information that sounds implausible, seek to verify it with others in the area or your real estate agent. Ideally, you want to buy a home that you love and that is located in an affordable area. The nicer the neighborhood, the longer your home will hold its value and appreciate.

OLDER HOME CONSIDERATIONS

If you are considering buying an older home with an attractive price tag, understand the repairs that will be necessary and the environmental issues. Older homes usually require more maintenance, so it will be helpful if you are handy with tools or can afford to pay for renovations.

You would be wise to hire a professional building inspector to check the home's structure and appliances, plus check for lead or radon problems. Homes built prior to 1978 could have lead-based paint, especially those homes built before 1960. Experts know that disturbing surfaces painted with lead-based paint creates lead dust. This dust can be an even greater danger than paint chips or peeling paint to children. Anyone can get lead poisoning, but children under seven are at the most risk because their bodies are easily damaged. Environmental experts can suggest ways to remove this type of paint safely. Check the library and your local newspaper for information.

NEGOTIATING THE FINE POINTS

Home purchases require patience and negotiation. If you are buying when lots of homes are available, commonly called "a buyer's market," you should definitely negotiate. There are so many points you can include in a purchase agreement to make it work for you. For instance you can negotiate to have appliances, fixtures, drapery, equipment, or furniture that is difficult to move included in the sale.

Always conceal your thrill when you fall in love with a home. Agents know that buyers who are hopelessly enthralled with a house tend to pay higher prices. They are pros at reading body language and signals between spouses. Your best bet is to make positive comments about every home that you see, but don't be overenthused about any. Watch your smiles and nods to your partner and save the comments for when you and your spouse are alone. Be very careful about disclosing your financial information. If you let the seller know your financial situation too early, it could affect your negotiation leverage.

Home warranty plans and home inspections are also excellent negotiating points. If sellers are anxious to move, they may pay for the entire warranty or inspection to hasten the close of the home sale. At the very least, they may split the cost with you. You do have the option to make

the sale contingent on a thorough inspection or warranty.

MAKING AN OFFER

When you find a house to your liking, think about it for a while. Move cautiously and deliberately in a home sale transaction. Ask your agent to give you "comps" (comparable house sales) on any house you're seriously considering, but don't take these at face value. Comps can help you to determine if the asking price is reasonable and to calculate an offer. If your offer is not accepted, you can counteroffer at small intervals.

When making an offer, be careful if the property you're buying is located in an older neighborhood with many different styles and price tags, or if it has been on the market for more than six months. Be especially careful not to pay too much for a house that has just gone up for sale. See the Real Estate Agents chapter for more information on offers and counteroffers.

It is imperative to have a title insurance company, real estate attorney, or title expert examine the title (with a legal description) to a property before you close on your home. A title search will confirm the legal owner of the property and how the property is held (joint tenancy, for example). Your purchase contract should include a contingency that allows you to inspect the title condition.

You also want to know if there are any restrictions that affect the property, such as covenants, conditions, and restrictions (CC&Rs) and easements that affect the property. Also be sure you know if any liens (loans, judgments, property taxes, mechanic's liens, or IRS tax liens) are recorded against the property. If you discover a title defect (called a "cloud") and the sellers can't remedy the situation by the closing date, the seller must return

Look for "Info-Line" services in the classified section of the local newspaper. These are provided by real estate companies and offer free information on almost any aspect of home sales transactions.

your deposit and you are released from the sales contract.

The Fair Housing Act of 1988 prohibits sellers from denying housing or rejecting an offer based on buyers' or renters' familial status. False advertisement is not allowed, nor can you be denied access to any Multiple Listing Service. Steering is also illegal. This includes directing people to other communities, discouraging the viewing of a house, or misrepresenting the home in question. There are a few exceptions to this law, so be sure and ask your broker about them if you have questions.

When you express interest in a particular house, you will receive a disclosure form that was filled out by the current homeowners. Carefully examine it. This form is a legal document that the homeowners were required to complete, revealing information about the home and noting any material issues that could affect the next homeowner. Several issues that are included on the form are the systems in the house, structural considerations (and changes), land boundaries, environmental issues, and neighborhood conditions.

BUYER REPRESENTATIVES AND BUYER BROKERS

It is a fact of life that real estate agents basically work for the people who are selling a home. Real estate agents cannot advise buyers what to offer for a property or reveal why the house is for sale without the seller's permission. So where does that leave you, the home buyer? Even with seller disclosure requirements (the seller must make you aware of any defects or problems in the home), home buyers need someone who is going to look out for their best interests.

Enter the buyer broker. Buyer brokers are professional representatives whose sole responsibility is to be loyal to home buyers

Call the National Association of Exclusive Buyer Agents (NAEBA) at (800) 986-2322 for free information on a qualified exclusive buyer broker in your area. If you cannot find an exclusive buyer agent in your area, check out www.smarthomesearch.org or call (800) 383-7188.

and help them make informed purchase decisions. Here are some good reasons to consider buyer brokers:

• They will negotiate to obtain the lowest price and best terms and conditions.

• They have accessibility to all of the homes for sale, including homes for sale by owners.

• They keep all buyer financial information confidential.

• They research the seller's motivation for selling, which can provide valuable information for negotiating a sale.

The majority of buyer agencies allow the buyer's agent fee to come out of the transaction amount. The listing agent and the buyer broker both receive a fee. If the brokers don't work under this arrangement, they ask for a flat fee or an hourly wage. An experienced buyer broker is well versed in property regulations and financing alternatives. A growing service, the buyer broker option is definitely worth looking into for your future home.

HOME OFFICE CONSIDERATIONS

More and more people are establishing an office in their home, either as entrepreneurs or because their employers are downsizing from office buildings and creating satellite workspaces for their employees. If you have a home office or think you may need one in the future, you have several considerations to factor into your home evaluation.

You will need to research the zoning laws and business permits before you buy or rent a place to live to see whether a home office is permissible. You have to think about what your daily schedule will be like, such as the number of hours you will spend in your home office, whether you will receive clients and deliveries, whether you need a separate entrance for the office, and whether the distance from common family areas will allow you the necessary privacy.

Consider what type and how much equipment you will need. Anticipate whether your business will grow, and if so, how much counter and workspace you will need. Check out the natural lighting in the morning and afternoon so you will know what kind of indoor lighting is necessary.

When you survey homes, keep these points in mind. If the house does not allow for the necessary space, think about whether the home could be renovated at a later date and the cost that would be involved in doing so. If a home office is a new endeavor for you, realize that renovations, equipment, supplies, space, and electricity are some of the expenses that can be used, partially or fully, as tax advantages. The rules for deductions are very specific and change yearly, so you should ask an accountant about the regulations to get the maximum tax benefit for the year in which you file your income tax.

HOME INSPECTIONS

It is important to have a home inspected before you sign a purchase agreement. More than 40 percent of previously owned homes for sale today have at least one serious defect, so this is a very prudent exercise for home buyers.

If you cannot negotiate the payment of an inspection, spend the money and have it done regardless, as it is a small cost compared with potentially thousands you could pay in repair and/or replacement costs for a defect in the home. The inspection should include the home's structure, electrical wiring, major appliances, plumbing and heating, air conditioning unit, and roof. Inquire about any water or mildew markings. See the Close-Up in this chapter for home inspection services for more information.

You need to engage a company that specifically does home inspections and accompany the inspector while he or she performs the service at your prospective home. Systems that should always be inspected include heating and cooling, electrical, and plumbing, as well as major appliances, walls, ceilings, insulation, and the roof. Call three inspection companies and compare their services and prices. Ask companies to send you literature about their services, specials, and specifics for the home you are considering.

Buying a home is one of the biggest financial decisions you will make. Hard as it may be, don't leave a house that you are interested in without being satisfied that you know as much about it as possible. Ask questions, observe, and take your time.

If your real estate representative cannot satisfactorily answer your questions, he or she should know where to get the details for you.

Having bought and sold many homes in our eighteen moves, we have (regretfully) overlooked some of the important points in this chapter. Whether the home you buy will be yours for one or for twenty years, your goal is to make a sound investment and be comfortable and happy in your home.

HOME PURCHASE ALTERNATIVES

If you plan to purchase a place to live in your new community but do not find an existing home that you truly love, there are alternatives for you to consider. One of these alternatives is building a new home, and the other is buying a condominium. People may consider these options because of retirement, changing household (fewer or more people living at home), or, simply, personal convenience.

Building is more challenging due to the fact that people are usually new to the area and do not know the preferred building sites, the builders, or the subcontractors. This issue will be addressed first, giving you an overview of the process, your options, ways to select a contractor, the costs and variables that are involved, and what to consider in land purchases. Following this section is information about buying and selling condominiums, as well as guidelines to evaluate them.

BUILDING OVERVIEW

Before you plunge into building, realize that it takes, on average, about 10 months to complete a home. Plus, you should allow an extra month or perhaps two in your schedule because delays can occur due to unforeseen problems such as inclement weather, construction delays, or material unavailability. If you require interim living arrangements, you must find short-term housing. Although finding short-term (less than a year) rentals is challenging, nego-

tiable leases do exist. Inquire at real estate agencies; if you are relocating for work, ask your company about available housing. These sources may know of a home that is unsold and whose owners would be happy to have the income of a partial year's rent. If possible, find temporary quarters that are convenient to your future home to give you easy access to the building site.

Building a home provides the unique opportunity to plan a dwelling to meet your family's needs and lifestyle. Homeowners who anticipate another move in a few years also find building attractive because up-to-date features and styling make homes easier to sell. Large, serviceable kitchens with upgraded appliances, large bathrooms with steam showers, oversized and custom-designed closets, great rooms, fireplaces, and decks are attractive to home buyers.

Begin your building efforts by speaking to at least three building contractors. Meet with the contractors to learn about their building plans, gain insight about current home styles, competitive costs, extra services, and details that you can expect to have included in a contract. Ask to see some of their house plans. If you want to make alterations in an existing plan, find out how willing they would be to accommodate you. Builders are often more amenable to negotiate options than base price (for instance, they would rather widen a walkway or finish a room than

If a builder seems eager to make a sale, the builder may have a large number of unsold homes. You can check the number of unsold units by looking at the map or project list in the builder's model or office.

decrease the price). If word circulates that a builder reduced a client's price, it would naturally affect future business.

You will be working closely with your builder for nine months to a year, so take your time in the evaluation process. Building a home can become very personal (discussing bathrooms and bedrooms, for instance) and it is important that you feel comfortable with the person of choice to develop a good working relationship. Your assessment should include the contractor's capabilities, costs, and home design options. Builders usually charge by the square foot; understand exactly what you can expect to receive for the fees charged. The agreed-upon price for your home and all costs and extras should be specifically outlined in your contract. If costs for a product (such as lumber) escalate during building, you do not want to be charged additional fees.

If a builder describes an available home as "new construction," find out whether construction took place without delay or remained only partially finished for a year or more waiting for a buyer. If a home was left standing and unfinished for many months, you should definitely take the precaution of having it professionally inspected. A structure that has been left standing will be more vulnerable to problems such as termites or rot. To investigate such problems, ask about the history of the project or do some research at the local public records office.

Coordinating the building schedule with your builder at the outset is another very important aspect in the building process. Your builder will outline a construction schedule for your home, and you need to be aware of your responsibilities in this schedule. There are many selections that you will need to make for your home, such as flooring, plumbing, tile, cabinetry and doors, hardware, appliances, and electrical fixtures. These items must be selected and ordered with enough time to spare so that the building schedule is not delayed.

To obtain land on which to build your home, you can purchase it from your builder or buy land on your own. Many builders have land sites that they are trying to develop. If a builder has land that is a relatively new building site, remember that as an early buyer you may have some negotiation leverage simply because builders typically want to show their houses are selling quickly. As an early buyer, you may be able to get more home for your money (the builder may add a few extras as an incentive to build). Keep in mind that you may have to assume some risk when moving into a new development. The risk will involve not knowing the pending price ranges for your development, as well as future home styles and sizes. It may be hard to discern when the area will be completely developed; as a result, it is possible you could end up living with mud and construction off and on for several years.

Another way to purchase land is to search the real estate section of the local newspaper for land that is for sale, land auctions, or foreclosures. If you are purchasing land outright, be sure that it meets the guidelines that are critical to obtain a mortgage. The land you choose should be safe environmentally and suitable for construction and development. Also, understand the real estate and property transfer taxes and the zoning ordinances. You surely do not want to find a few years down the road that your new home could be adjacent to an apartment or shopping complex or business offices. Last, but certainly not least, whether you have children or not, realize that homes in excellent school districts hold more value.

THE HOUSE PLAN

Most people who build start with their own idea of a working house plan. For instance, they usually want to incorporate the same types of living areas and rooms they enjoy and spend the most time in. Builders usually have home plans already laid out that you can use as they are or alter to meet your needs. Or you could have a plan designed that is entirely unique for you. A very experienced builder may complete the latter, or you may have to engage an architect.

The house plan deserves a lot of time. Don't rush into building before you have carefully evaluated each room to see whether it will accommodate your furniture and your day-to-day activities. As you lay out the floor plan, furniture measurements take on a whole new meaning. Your goal is to consider your furniture layout very carefully. If you have to move doors, windows, or enlarge a room in your house plans, it is a lot easier to do so on paper. After building begins, moving walls to accommodate furniture or living space is either very expensive or impossible. Also, give some thought to what your lifestyle will be like in five to ten years. Your family could increase or decrease, or you could start a business or work at home in some capacity. Think about how these changes will affect the space and plans of the home you are building now.

SAVINGS TO CONSIDER

Some ways you can save money when you build a home are by doing some of the

If there are many new condominiums in your prospective area, be skeptical about the complexes that are drastically increasing their number of units, especially if they are not increasing their services.

work on your own. The amount of work you choose to do will depend directly on your own capabilities and the time you have available to do the work. In the first home we built, we did all the painting and the majority of the paper hanging. We found that we could move through our home fairly quickly, painting walls and ceilings prior to carpeting and furnishing the home. Keep in mind that you can also complete an unfinished area at a later date, rather than have the builder do the work. If gardening is your hobby, you can purchase small bushes and trees at local garden centers and plant them yourself. If you require larger trees as well, you can pay a professional nursery to plant them. And, last, buying your own land is sometimes less costly than purchasing it from a builder.

CONDOMINIUMS: ANOTHER ALTERNATIVE

If you must purchase a place to live and do not have the time nor the inclination to build a home, another alternative is to purchase a condominium. There are many reasons why condominium living is the perfect choice for some people. These may be due to an increase in your travel schedule, a decrease in your "at-home" family, decreased mobility, or simply because you are at a stage in your life when you don't want the maintenance responsibilities of a home. Your responsibilities as a condominium owner usually include only the interior maintenance of your unit.

Condominiums are increasing in popularity. This is a direct reflection of changing

CLOSE-UP

Advantages and Disadvantages of Condominium Ownership

Advantages:

1. Owners vote on association council member selection.
2. Room sizes within a unit often match those of single-family homes.
3. Monthly fees typically include trash hauling, water/sewer service, and cable TV.
4. Limited unit access means more safety and less traffic.
5. Association provides lawn care.
6. Repairs for the routine maintenance of the exteriors of the unit are covered in the homeowner's dues.

Disadvantages:

1. Sharing common space with other tenants sacrifices some privacy.
2. Maintenance of amenities and facilities adds to the monthly fee.
3. Association guidelines typically limit personal preferences for outside features, such as painting your front door your favorite color.
4. Units may be close to noisy neighbors.
5. You are dependent upon the response of the association for unit repairs.
6. You must budget for monthly fees to cover routine upkeep.

lifestyles in the United States, such as the increase in two-income families, greater longevity, and more single-parent households. These units afford ownership of a private dwelling, room sizes that are comparable to single-family homes, and less outside maintenance.

There seems to be a surplus of condominiums in some areas. This is both positive and negative. The good news is that it is creating more of a buyer's market; therefore, you have more negotiating power when you purchase one. The downside, of course, is that if you have to sell your unit, the large number of condominiums makes the sale more challenging.

Before you purchase a condominium unit, think about features that will be good for yourself, as well as for future resale. As you visit different complexes, note whether the units and grounds are well maintained and attractive. Some condominium features that will help you to make a wise purchase include attractive floor plan, well-lighted parking areas, and good exterior maintenance.

Most condominium complexes have homeowner associations with personnel to oversee the operation and rentals of their condominium units. Typically, the respective association is responsible for the care of the common areas (outside grounds and facilities). The association charges a fee for its services, and these services are often included in your monthly condominium fees. When you compare units, make sure the association fees that are included cover the amenities (such as the pool or clubhouse) that you will use and enjoy. You want to avoid paying for facilities or services that will never be of value to you.

Homeowner associations occasionally stipulate the exterior colors, materials, planters, styling, and types of additions (such as a deck) that are allowed. Be sure you understand all the rules and regulations that apply to your unit and know your responsibilities within the complex. It is a good idea to talk to other owners in the complex and to ask them how promptly and satisfactorily the association attends to residents' problems, how often the homeowner dues are increased, and whether assessments are forthcoming. Furthermore, if problems should develop at some point between neighbors within the condominium community, most associations will act as a go-between on the owner's behalf.

SELLING A CONDOMINIUM

If you are transferred in a year or find that you have to sell your unit for other reasons, be sure to make your condominium unique (such as with decorations or special lighting). The tips in the Negotiating a Profitable Home Sale chapter can help you to prepare your condominium unit for sale as well. When pricing a unit to sell, be aware of what you can realistically expect for the unit so that it is priced right the first time. You cannot afford to waste time and possibly lose a sale because your unit is inappropriately priced. The value of condominiums fluctuates, just as that of homes, due to supply and demand within the existing market.

RENTING—PROS AND CONS

Buying a home and owning land have always been the American dream. Today, however, we see an increase of dual-career couples, changing lifestyles, and different employer perspectives about purchasing real estate. Many people are reevaluating their choice of dwellings, and renting is no longer considered a second cousin to buying a home. Sometimes it is even preferable.

Some individuals are choosing to rent because they want the flexibility that renting affords them. Some perhaps lost money on a recent home sale. Others are encouraged by their employers to rent because it costs the company less to move them. And some people simply do not want the responsibility of owning a home.

If you are planning to rent a dwelling, this chapter outlines safety, financial, and lifestyle issues for you to consider.

APARTMENT EVALUATION

You surely don't want to get stuck in an apartment in which you will hear the next-door neighbor's music when you want to go to sleep or where children may be playing and making their usual amount of noise if you work at home during the day. It is important to visit a unit you are considering during different times of the day to assess these issues.

Consider also whether children are allowed in the apartment complex. Even if you presently do not have a child, think about whether you could be starting a family before your lease runs out.

Evaluate the financial outlay required, including the rent plus the upkeep and utility costs. You will need an apartment where these costs don't amount to more than your paycheck. Also consider the stability of your current salary.

Other issues to put into your evaluation are whether or not you may have to move again in the near future. Would the lease for the apartment you are considering allow you to sublease or to break your commitment without undue penalty?

Do you know whether or not your furniture will fit in the rooms? Don't end up on moving day with the terrible realization that you will have to rent an additional storage space (which is expensive) for excess furniture or sell pieces you might not want to part with.

Safety is also very important while you are living in the apartment, as well as when you are walking, driving, or parking. Especially think about locks for windows, mailboxes, and dead-bolt locks for doors. If these features do not exist, ask to have them included in your agreement. Know if the locks have been changed in between

When considering a rental, calculate how the rental rates compare with homes in the area where you are looking.

tenants. Check on smoke detectors (required by law), a fire extinguisher, and accessible fire exits. Visit the complex during the evening to see how well the entryways and parking lots are lighted.

And, finally, consider whether the complex offers recreational amenities that are enticing to you. The difference can be huge; some complexes practically imitate health and social clubs, while others have only the bare minimum or no amenities at all.

Be sure that you know the distances to places to which you must travel every day, as well as distances from physicians, hospitals, transportation, and favorite pastimes. (If your health club is forty minutes away as opposed to ten minutes, you will probably use it less.)

LEASE AGREEMENTS

Any lease is a binding contract. Read the agreement form thoroughly, and if there is a clause that you do not understand, ask the landlord to explain it to you or seek legal counsel before you sign on the dotted line. Never sign any lease with blank spaces to be filled in later. Details of all agreements between you and your landlord need to be outlined in writing prior to

signing. Each party should have a copy of this agreement.

A few aspects that should be clearly stated in the lease agreement include the names of the tenant and landlord, correct address, the amount of rent and due date, the length of the lease, and the stipulations to renew a lease. Know also who is responsible for repairs and utilities. Leases can vary for many reasons—the type and location of the dwelling, the security deposits, the financial information requested, the availability of new tenants, the housing market, and the season of the year.

An oral lease is a spoken (verbal) agreement between the landlord and the tenant. In some states an oral agreement is legal, but not in all states; therefore, verify this before proceeding. If it is legal, an oral lease typically runs from month to month. Naturally you are dependent on each person remembering the agreement in exactly the same way. If there is a disagreement, and you only have an oral lease, a judge must decide the outcome.

The most important component of a lease is that the tenant knows what is expected of him or her and what responsibilities the landlord has. Any lease that you sign should indicate that the landlord has repair work completed before you move into the apartment, or at a promised date afterward. It should then specify the amount of rent you can withhold if you are inconvenienced or if the work is not completed as agreed upon.

Some of the biggest areas of contention between a tenant and a landlord are who is responsible, and in what way, for repairs and maintenance. Appliances can be a big issue, as well as electrical repairs. Typically the landlord assumes responsibility for these repairs, primarily from a safety standpoint. Another area for dispute is pet ownership. If pets are allowed, landlords must have specific guidelines in the lease for such things as leash rules, areas where pets can be walked, and the responsibility of cleaning up after your pet. If your lease states that pets are not allowed, don't push your luck and acquire one after you move into the apartment.

Yes, you can negotiate. If there are numerous units for rent in the complex you are considering (10 percent or more), negotiate! Just as with buying a home or condominium, there are areas that can be negotiated in rental agreements, especially if the landlord is anxious to fill the unit. You can negotiate one month's free rent; new or refurbished appliances; new paint and/or paper; free pool access; new carpeting; or a shorter lease. These are just a few of those issues; you may think of others when you survey the complex you are considering, or consider your personal situation.

When you approach your rental agent to fill out an application, be sure you are prepared. Take along your Social Security card, references, bank account number, driver's license, present address and telephone number, and the name and address of your employer. Letters of reference (from your employer or former bank man-

ager) may also help your credibility, especially in a large city where landlords could require more documentation.

All housing units require constant upkeep. Be sure to follow the rules and take care of your responsibilities, such as reporting problems as soon as they occur and abiding by the contract agreement. The landlord typically performs repairs. If you would like to make alterations to the apartment itself, discuss these with your landlord. Relatively minor changes like painting the walls a neutral color may be allowed, whereas adding track lighting may not. If the interior is not satisfactory, ask to have specific changes you would like to make included in the lease. Know that you probably won't be able to take those with you unless they can be removed without damage or noticeable marks.

If you are renting from individuals (not company-owned complexes), you should be extra careful about what is included in the lease. When an apartment is someone's personal property, he or she may be less flexible in negotiations.

RENTALS—YOUR RIGHTS AND RESPONSIBILITIES

Thoroughly check the entire apartment before signing a lease. List all defects and damages and document them with pictures. Develop the film requesting two sets of prints, and do so immediately, so the photos are dated. Send a set (with a polite letter) to the landlord to avoid deduction of unwarranted repairs from your security deposit. Although this may sound like overkill, horror stories are common with loose or verbal agreements. Take a few precautions at the outset, and you will be patting yourself on the back if a problem arises down the road.

Check the section of your lease that deals with terminating the lease. If you need to break a lease, you must know what you are responsible for financially. A clause in the lease may permit you to sublease a dwelling, but if the person who you lease to damages the property, you could be held accountable.

Landlords do not have the right to enter your apartment any time they wish. Instead, they should make an appointment with you to do so. If it is necessary for the landlord to enter your apartment for any reason (usually only for an emergency), a note should be left indicating that someone was in your unit and for what purpose. Anything else is considered trespassing.

If a problem develops, first check with your neighbors to make sure you are not the only one experiencing it. Then immediately inform your landlord in writing about the problem. Make two copies of your complaint, ask the landlord to initial one copy, and keep it for your records. If after one week (depending on the problem) the repairs are not made or you are not satisfied, you can consider alternative measures. You can sometimes withhold rent legally or, if you repair the problem, you can deduct the repair costs from your next rental payment. You can also report

the problem to the Health Department in your town if you believe that is necessary. There are three other avenues of assistance commonly used by apartment dwellers. These are the local bar association, the local landlord group, or a local legal firm.

The landlord's insurance policy does not cover your personal property, clothes, furniture, or valuables. Be sure you are adequately covered by renter's insurance, which also protects you against unpredictable losses due to fire or smoke, vandalism or theft, and storms.

ROOMMATES

If you share an apartment with a roommate, be sure you know what you are liable for if this person leaves without paying his or her full share of the rent and apartment costs. If you have a friend in need of lodging and this person just wants to "bunk in for a while," be sure you have the landlord's permission. You need to understand what constitutes a temporary guest and when this guest takes on the status of resident. The landlord can legally ask for more rent if another person lives with you. Be sure you know your landlord's rules about this.

ADJUSTING TO YOUR NEW COMMUNITY

Many people associate culture shock with moving to another country. Surprisingly enough, you can experience culture shock by moving only a very short distance. A move from the northeastern part of the United States to the Southwest, or from a small suburban area to a large city, can be very challenging and dramatic cultural change. The pre-move visit should have prepared you with information to use early on. Once you arrive in the new city, continue to learn as much as possible about it. The tips in this chapter are designed to help you feel at home and quickly settle in to any community.

EARLY STEPS

Before you unpack those hundreds of boxes (the same boxes that took four movers three days to pack), use any spare time that you have and become the proverbial tourist. The more you tour the city, the more comfortable you will feel in your new surroundings.

Visit the Chamber of Commerce or local information bureau to find out what museums, theaters, and events are nearby. Pick up a city map and telephone directory if you don't already have one. Check to see if there is an *Insiders' Guide* to the city. The entire family can get involved in the quest of scouting out their favorite pastimes, services, and entertainment.

Show your children their schools and meet their teachers as well. Be sure to locate the bus stops and rehearse the routes that your children will be using to and from your home. Children will need to have your new office name, address, and telephone number and have people who can be backup contacts in case you cannot be reached.

Subscribe to the local newspaper to learn about the city, merchants, services, and school news. The paper will also help you to become familiar with the overall tone of your new community.

Get acquainted with important services. Visit your bank to meet with personnel and set up a safe-deposit box. Stop by the post office near your home and introduce yourself. Be sure to check that the personnel has your proper forwarding information for your mail and know your timing for moving into your home.

This is a good time to arrange for services to be established at your new home. If you have small children, it will be wonderful to have television services available, especially if you experience inclement weather on moving day.

Find as many positive aspects to your new city as possible. It will take several

---

Visit with the new teachers about one month after your children have started school. A personal visit will help you to learn about any concerns early on.

Safety Tips

1. Be aware of the level of safety in your new area and use well-traveled routes. You or your children may be able to travel more (or less) freely than the last place you lived.
2. Inform a family member of your travel plans, the route, and how to contact you if you do not arrive as expected.
3. Memorize telephone numbers and street addresses for your new home and office.
4. Have your registration card and insurance card (with a contact for the insurance agent) with you when you travel.
5. Have one or two practice routes planned to exit your new home in case of a fire. Be sure that your children know the drill.
6. Everyone in the family should know where the fuse box, utility meters, alarm system, furnace/thermostat, and water and gas shut-off are located and how to operate them.
7. Install dead-bolt locks on all outside doors and the door to your garage, and secure sliding glass doors with a locking bar.
8. Do not hide keys outside your home.

months to adjust, but you will feel more at home as you make an effort to become active and involve your family within the community.

MEDICAL CARE

One of the most important details you need to attend to as soon as possible in a new area is to locate the medical care your family requires. Locate medical facilities and pharmacies, and if you have referrals for doctors and dentists, find their offices as well. Compatibility with a physician is very important, so set up an appointment to meet with prospective doctors before the time comes that you need their care.

When evaluating medical care and doctors, consider accessibility, diversity of services, qualifications, and whether the physician and his or her associated hospital accepts your insurance coverage. It is important that the physician you choose be "board certified," which indicates that the doctor regularly passes a rigorous oral and written examination. If you live near a teaching hospital, call and ask about local physicians. Some doctors recommend calling specialists for information about finding a primary care physician.

You also need to be concerned with your health insurance carrier because your policy may dictate the medical care providers and services that are available to you. If you have a PPO (Preferred Provider Organization) that contracts for services with individual physicians, you can choose from a list of doctors. There is usually an extra charge if you visit doctors outside of the organization.

Medications and pharmacies are a very important part of a well-rounded medical program. Everyone in your family should be familiar with his or her own prescription medications and their side effects, especially if someone has a condition that requires special medications or care.

SETTLING IN

The success of any relocation is directly proportional to the effort that is put into it, as well as the relocating family's attitude and perspective. Especially consider that the relocation process is always challenging for children. Your children must know that they are being considered in the entire moving process. During the early months in your new location, it is important to have routine family discussions during which you can address any problems or situations that may surface among your family. Listen very carefully to what you believe might be the "real" issues for your child. Often what underlies resistance is simply fears of the unknown that parents can talk about and handle with care. Remember, whatever you as parents are feeling is magnified in your children.

The most important aspect of relocating is to evaluate everything that pertains to the move and how a move will affect you and your family at this time in your life. Make an effort to join clubs, get involved, and learn something new about your new community every week. I wish you all the best in your new home.

PART II:
VOLUNTARY RELOCATION

WHERE WOULD YOU *LIKE* TO LIVE?

The first half of this book details the nuts and bolts of relocating primarily because of business or employment requirements. These moves are made not necessarily because a family *wants* to relocate but because relocation is *required*. Part II of this book focuses on *voluntary* relocation. When you control the decisions as to where you will be going and when you will be moving, new sets of strategies and decisions come into play.

When your employer transfers you to a job in another city or if your company is relocating to another state, you had better relocate if you value your job. These things happen with such frequency that some families become expert at marketing their houses in one town while buying in the new community, transferring home bases without missing a beat. They soon learn the ins and outs of efficient packing, dealing with moving companies, settling their children into a new school, and handling other details.

Then there are those who want to relocate to another town or to another state simply because they want to do so. There's an enormous difference between moving to a new community because you *have* to and moving there because you *want* to. Voluntary relocation makes good sense when one or more family members lose their jobs and no satisfactory replacement jobs can be found in the area. Maybe you are simply sick and tired of living in a stuffy midwestern town and would like to find a high-paying job in a semitropical beach community where you can go deep-sea fishing any time you and your husband feel like it. Maybe you're retiring from a lifetime of work, and you and your soul mate long for a new lifestyle and new friends in a different part of the country. Or perhaps you don't *have* to work because you are fortunate to have enough income to get by without working and would like a change in scene, to take some college classes, or to enjoy big-city theater and museums for a change. Should any of the above be the case, you may see no advantage in remaining where you are, so this could be the time to shop around for an interesting and appropriate locale to create a new beginning and a new style of living.

MAKING LIFE-CHANGING DECISIONS

When your employer decides that you should relocate, or you have a great job

When you relocate voluntarily, you have a marvelous opportunity to make a totally new start. You no longer have to live where your job dictates. You have a chance to select your ideal climate, the type of community that appeals to you, and the sports and hobbies you've always wanted to try. When relocating, think "new lifestyles!"

offer in another city, the major decision has already been made. You know where you are going and when you have to be there. You put your home on the market, begin packing things you will keep, and start selling or discarding items you won't need. You'll probably start negotiating to buy or rent a home in your new destination as soon as you get your moving orders, maybe before you even visit your new hometown. It's possible that your employer will have made housing arrangements for you, in which case you may not set eyes on your future home until you arrive, following the moving van.

When you are relocating voluntarily, the technical details and physical chores of moving come *last*. First comes the process of researching possible relocation destinations and selecting your new hometown. You have to decide not only *where* you will relocate but also *when* and *if* you will relocate. This decision can have a profound effect on your family's future lifestyle and should not be approached lightly. For example, children growing up and going to school in Chicago will experience life differently and will have dissimilar worldviews from those growing up in San Diego. (For one thing, they don't need surfboards in Chicago.) You and your spouse, with input from the children, have the opportunity of choosing lifestyles that match your intellectual and recreational interests and the climate that suits you best.

When *you* decide that it would be a good idea to relocate, the task becomes more complicated. You begin with an assessment of all the possible places where you might want to live. If you will be changing employers or finding a new one, you may need to investigate job possibilities by visiting the community to make applications and, of course, to see if you like the place. If you have school-age chil-

dren, you'll need to know something about the school system in the various towns to decide which might be best for the children, as well as which neighborhood would be most convenient. Housing prices and the cost of living enter into the picture and could determine or eliminate relocation prospects. You can even change your mind at any point during your search and decide *not* to relocate should you not find the ideal place for relocation.

CHOOSING YOUR NEW HOMETOWN

One major point that cannot be overstated is that *you must do your own research to find your new community for relocation*. Feature articles in magazines and newspapers often tempt you with articles titled something like, "The Twenty Best Towns in the U.S.A." When you turn to these articles for guidance, you'll notice that rarely do writers agree which are the "best" towns because each list is different. If these were truly the twenty best towns in the country, wouldn't there be some agreement? You quickly realize that many articles are opinions of writers who, in all likelihood, have never visited these towns but have done their research by using statistics and descriptions freely found in libraries or on the Internet.

These writers rank their "best towns" on a scale from one to twenty, as if they were rating football teams. With a football team we can check the statistics and past performances; cities and towns don't receive scores except in the writer's mind. The fact that a writer likes a city and ranks it number one in his or her magazine article doesn't prove a thing.

The problem with ranking communities is that favorable ratings are awarded on the basis of conditions that do not affect everyone. What may be favorable for one

CLOSE-UP

Community Features to Check Out

In our opinion, the items below are essential features of a viable community. Your needs and preferences most likely are different from ours, so feel free to add or subtract from the checklist.

1. A comfortable climate: Temperatures and weather patterns should match your lifestyle. Will you be tempted to go outdoors and exercise in any season, or will harsh winters and suffocating summers confine you to an indoor life?

2. Affordable housing: Is quality housing available at a price you're willing and able to pay? Are neighborhoods visually pleasing and free of pollution and traffic snarls?

3. Jobs and/or volunteer opportunities: If you plan on working, is the employment picture OK? If you are retiring, will you find interesting volunteer jobs or paid jobs (if that's what you want) to satisfy your need to keep busy?

4. Recreation and hobbies: Does your relocation choice provide recreational opportunities such as sports, arts centers, adult education, fishing, hunting, or whatever else interests you and your family?

5. Friendly and accepting community: Will you find common interests with your neighbors? Will you fit in and make friends easily? Will you find friends with your own cultural, social, and political background? Is this important to you?

6. Reasonable cost of living: Are goods and services reasonably priced? Will you be able to afford to hire help from time to time when you need to? Will your income be high enough to be significantly affected by state income taxes? Will property taxes make a big difference?

7. Adequate medical care: Do local physicians accept new patients? Does the area have an adequate hospital? Does a family member have a medical problem requiring a specialist?

8. Distance from family and friends: Are you going to be relocating too far away for people to visit from time to time?

9. Local transportation: Does your new community have bus transportation? Most small towns have none, which makes you totally dependent on an automobile or taxi service. Is this important to you? How far is the nearest airport with airline connections?

10. Personal safety: Can you walk through your neighborhood without fearful glances over your shoulder? Will you feel OK about leaving your home for a vacation without dreading a break-in?

family can be deadly for yours. For example, high employment and a booming business climate will boost a town's popularity rating for those looking for employment, whereas others might not like the region's harsh weather, high taxes, or congestion. Quality grammar schools and juvenile recreational programs are a plus for families with kids, but retirees are more concerned with quality restaurants, continuing education programs, and safe neighborhoods. Cultural amenities, such as museums and operas, can boost a community's rank very high in some folks' relocation analysis. Yet how many times a month will you be visiting a museum? How often do you go to the opera? Would you rather live in a town with ten golf courses and no museums, or ten museums and no golf courses? Would more golf courses increase a town's ranking for you if you don't play golf?

To find your ideal location, you're going to have to do your own ranking. The rest of this book guides you through this process of discovery.

RELOCATING TO FIND WORK

Deciding to move from your hometown to take a new job can be a thrilling, life-changing event. Making the decision is like standing at a crossroads with paths veering off in several directions, knowing that each path will take you someplace really nice, and each place will change your future in different, unpredictable ways. I recall once, early in my career, when I had three job offers: one in Florida, one in Nevada, and one in Michigan. As my wife and our children discussed the possibilities of each direction to travel, we felt a growing excitement and a sense of adventure. We chose to move to Ann Arbor, Michigan. Later we often considered how different our lives would have turned out had I accepted a job in Key West or in Las Vegas instead. The possibilities are unlimited.

Not everyone looks upon a relocation with enthusiasm and a sense of adventure. Some are frightened by the challenge of leaving friends and family and venturing into a totally new environment. The final decision could involve much soul-searching as well as research. Examine your reasons for leaving. You may have no choice because of your employment situation, because you need a better climate for health reasons, or because you are retiring and want to move to your dream location. Leaving family behind is one of the more powerful reasons not to move. Another powerful reason is a split in the family's desire to move, when only one person is in favor and the others are dreading the move.

CHANGING EMPLOYMENT

One excellent motive for considering relocation is to find employment when you've lost your job—or you hate your job—and your hometown cannot provide a satisfactory replacement. You have two choices: either lower your expectations and accept whatever local employment is available or look for a job in another community. If your lost job was with a large corporation, there's a third choice: You might successfully apply for a transfer to another city. If the latter strategy works out, and your family finds the new city acceptable, your problems are solved, and you can revisit the first part of this book for advice on how to proceed with relocation. Otherwise you'll need to do a community search as well as a job search.

When tracking tax-deductible expenses from your job-hunting efforts, keep a portfolio to hold a detailed logbook that records the date and time of everyone you talk to about employment. Record all of your expenses in the logbook. In the portfolio keep all receipts that could be relevant. Even the cost of the Insiders' Guide to Relocation *is deductible!*

Job search strategies vary among different trades and professions. Clearly, you know a lot more about where jobs in your line of work might be found and how to apply for them than any hints we can provide. Sometimes going through an employment agency or a "headhunter" is the accepted practice. Other times sending out your résumé will do the job. Often the only way is to apply in person because some companies never advertise new or vacant positions; they depend on employees to move into the job or to recommend friends.

Don't make the mistake of applying only to the larger corporations for employ-

CLOSE-UP

Tax Benefits for Job Searches

When your employer makes the decisions as to when and where you move, some or all of the expenses are often covered by the company. Some companies budget between $30,000 to $50,000 to move an employee's household. The expenses not covered by the company can often be written off your income for tax purposes. When you are relocating on your own, you can also deduct many expenditures for traveling around the country to look for that new job.

Before we go any further, please understand that tax laws and regulations are always changing and being reinterpreted. So be sure and consult your tax adviser for the latest rules and regulations. Having said this, below are the rules as we understand them.

Visiting the prospective communities for job interviews is usually considered a deductible expense and can amount to big bucks. These employment searches can be deductible provided you are looking for another job in the same line of work that you are now doing or were doing before you lost your job. It doesn't matter if you don't get the job, or at the last minute you decide not to take the job; if you have legitimate expenses—such as mileage (at 36.5 cents per mile), parking expenses, tolls, transportation, meals and entertainment, hotels bills, and so on— they can be deducted from your income. It is important to keep detailed records and all receipts, no matter how small. There are caveats with which your tax preparer can help you. For example, your expenses must be more than your standard deduction, or else there is no point in claiming them. There also are income restrictions should your income be in a high bracket.

Be aware that some conditions can disqualify you from taking job-hunting deductions (although they won't disqualify you from taking moving expenses). If you're looking for your *first* job, if you are looking for employment in a new line of work, or if you are researching a new business or relocating your business, you may not take a job-hunting deduction. This last item can be taken care of as business expenses and credited against your business income on Schedule C of your income tax filings. Again, the advice of a tax-savvy expert is needed here.

ment. Remember that with the general shift toward globalization, many large corporations are relocating production facilities and other jobs to foreign locations.

Do not overlook the classified section of the target community's newspaper. However, do not depend on this because while classified ads may be published, they may not appear in the hometown newspaper. It turns out that many companies—especially those seeking help in high-tech, computer, or other specialized professions—regularly place ads in newspapers located in major cities where workers tend to be concentrated, such as California's Silicon Valley, Boston, Seattle, or Austin, Texas. When a company needs a high-tech worker, it knows there will be more applicants in the large pool of workers found in these areas. You might check your library for newspapers from cities such as those mentioned. You could be surprised to find a job advertised for your potential relocation town in an out-of-state newspaper.

Internet job boards for your profession or trade can often be found by using an Internet search engine or by subscribing from a newsgroup browser. Internet Web pages from your target relocation town often yield information about businesses, industries, and potential employers, complete with addresses, telephone numbers, and e-mail contacts. (There's more about Internet use later in this section of the book.) If you are a professional, it's always possible that your college alumni association will have a networking system or a career center to help with your search. Your professional associations can be of great assistance—but you probably already know that.

Another possibility for obtaining an out-of-state job in your line of work is approaching an employee search firm,

commonly referred to as a headhunter. These search firms almost always specialize in one particular type of occupation or in a specific industry. You need to find out which ones are appropriate for you; applying to the wrong headhunter will result in a nonresponse to your résumé. One way to learn is to make inquiries at the personnel office of companies where you make your job applications. Ask whether this firm uses a headhunter's services and get the phone number or e-mail address. Your library might have a copy of the *Directory of Executive Recruiters* (Kennedy Publications, Fitzwilliam, New Hampshire), which can guide you to an agency that specializes in your field. You can also access the directory online at www.kennedyinfo.com/js/der.html. Another online source is *Recruiting Search Report* at www.rsronline.com.

RETRAINING FOR A NEW LINE OF WORK

For some workers employment can be difficult to find because technology is phasing out their skills. Others may find jobs scarce because the jobs they perform are being shifted overseas. Should either of these be the case, now may be the time to retrain, to learn new skills. Check with your local economic development office for possible state or federal assistance in acquiring your training for a new job field. The government may even pay you to learn a new profession or trade!

Community colleges often offer courses devoted to job preparation and retraining, usually with nominal and affordable tuition fees. You can choose from a variety of fields such as nursing, court reporting, accounting, automobile repair, and restaurant cooking. Depending on the college and the state, classes for nonresidents can be much more expensive; therefore, it may be wise to take your classes where you are living now and be ready for relocation, rather than move first and be hit with high out-of-state fees.

Some skills, such as nursing, teaching, and construction, are usually an asset no matter where you go, but some professions or trades may not be needed in the towns you have targeted as your relocation destination. You'll have to do some job research. One way to do this is by contacting state and local chambers of commerce, community colleges, business schools, universities, and trade associations to learn whether your skills are marketable in the geographic area you've selected.

RELOCATING FOR RETIREMENT

The most common reason for voluntarily relocation is retirement. Contrary to common belief, most retirees do *not* move from their hometowns or to another part of the country when they drop out of the workplace. After decades of living near family and socializing with old friends and neighbors, a move can be an upsetting and often unnecessary event. Studies have shown that those with the closest family ties and who are the most active in community affairs are those who are least likely to relocate when retiring. But, when retirement time comes, many recognize that their children and grandkids are scattered all over the continent and that most of their friends are people they work with who will become strangers once the retirees are out of the loop.

Retirees enjoy the widest range of relocation choices because job considerations don't enter into the picture in any big way. If you or your spouse plan on working during retirement, you'll find part-time jobs much easier to find than full-time positions, so you'll wait until after you settle into your new hometown before looking. This allows you the freedom to concentrate on such things as climate, recreational opportunities, cost of living, and other criteria that can affect your new lifestyle. Your larger concerns will be with issues such as how far you live from the golf course or the shopping mall instead of how far you have to commute to work. Another nonworry is

locating near good schools—your kids are grown and working in some other part of the country. In fact, retirees often make their relocation plans to be closer to their scattered children.

When voluntarily relocating to another community, retirees can be picky about items such as the cost of living, levels of property and state income taxes, the kind of neighbors they will have, crime levels, and other such factors.

A favorable cost-of-living community with affordable real estate prices can be crucial for retirees with limited budgets or for those who want to live well within their means. When researching low-cost communities, however, keep in mind that you'll often discover negative reasons why an area is low-cost. In some towns the most exciting thing to do is sit on the front porch and swat flies. Wages are another factor: low cost of living, inexpensive housing, and low wages tend to go hand in hand. For retirees, this is a double-edged sword. On the one hand, it means if you want to work part-time, you'll compete with $5.00-an-hour workers for jobs. On the other hand, when you need someone to work on your roof or to mow your lawn, you won't have to get a bank loan to pay the wages.

PLANNING AHEAD

Sometimes people put off making retirement decisions until just before they are ready to pull the plug on their job. They simply assume that Florida, Arizona, or California will be their retirement destinations without analyzing exactly why this should be. Perhaps most of their friends took that retirement route and they simply plan to follow suit. Some newly retired couples have followed their friends to sunny Florida, only to realize they've made a mistake after they've settled in. So they pack up and go somewhere else. There are so many of these moves that retirement experts refer to them as "Florida J-turns."

This is not to imply that Florida is a poor choice for retirement. On the contrary, for many people Florida is the perfect place for retirement because it offers exactly the lifestyle they dreamed of all those years when they were plugging away at their jobs, shoveling snow, and chipping ice from their windshields. The point is, Florida is not the *only* place in the entire country to consider for retirement—why not do your research and pick the place that matches your ideal requirements?

We once interviewed a couple from the Midwest who related some mistakes in their retirement planning process. First of all, they put off doing any research or planning until after the job ended. They didn't think detailed planning was necessary because they owned a large motor home and planned to use it to leisurely zero in on their ideal destination. It seemed logical— they would travel around for six months or a year until they found the perfect retirement hometown. They sold their home, packed up the motor home, and drove away, intending to travel the country for at least six months, trying out every likely town until they were satisfied with their final selection. Four days later they found themselves in Sedona, Arizona. The scenery was so spectacular, the winter climate so invigorating, they *knew* they had

found the perfect spot! So they traded their motor home and some cash for a deluxe, doublewide mobile home. They lost money, but they figured it was worth it. After they settled in, they realized they had made a mistake. It seems the wife had a medical condition, not very serious, but one that demanded the services of a specialist. They discovered that the nearest doctor was in Phoenix, a four-hour round trip, twice a week. After two months, it made sense to move closer to the doctor, so they sold their mobile home (for another loss) and bought a home in an adult community in Phoenix. Two months later, summer weather struck. The ovenlike temperatures—climbing above 100 degrees, day after sweltering day—proved that they had made yet another mistake. When we met them, they were living in a lovely home in Oregon's Rogue River Valley, but they were trying to sell because they were too far from the city and they discovered that they missed having lots of neighbors.

START THE PROCESS EARLY

Ideally you will start your retirement research early. A great way to do this is by combining research with vacations. Statistics show that couples who vacation at the same place several years in a row are more likely to relocate there upon retirement. That's fine, but instead of visiting the same place each year, try different parts of the country. You might find a new town much more to your liking. Between your home and your vacation destination, pause for a while whenever you encounter a particularly charming community. Check out the area as a possible place to live. Stay in a motel for a couple of days. Look at real estate, medical care, and recreation. Talk to local residents and see how they feel about living there.

Ask yourselves some questions: Will you find the kinds of cultural events you will enjoy? Cultural events can be anything from concerts, lectures, and stage plays to square-dance lessons, barbecues, and bowling tournaments. What about outdoor recreation to match your personality? Depending upon your needs, outdoor recreation could be anything from bicycling and tennis to hiking and sunbathing. For some, outdoor recreation could mean an open-air beer garden (in which case, relocating in a "dry" county would be a bad idea!). Ask yourselves, Would we be happy living here?

Before you decide that your favorite vacation town on the Carolina coast or that lovely resort in the Arizona desert is the perfect place, make a visit during the off-season before investing in your dream home. You may be stunned to discover that the town has a completely different personality once seasonal residents have all checked out and returned to their regular homes. Those natives who remain may convince you that you have nothing in common with them whatsoever. Those nice restaurants you loved to go to for dinner are closed for the season. Even many fast-food places are closed. Only those businesses selling the necessities remain open for limited hours. As for that wonderful weather—well, you could soon find out why they refer to this town as "seasonal" when the desert sun turns the countryside into a pizza oven, or how lonely the beach can be when frigid winds whip the surf to a frenzy.

A friend of ours from Chicago made a visit to California during January and was totally amazed at the gorgeous, sunny weather of an oceanside community south of San Francisco. The golf course was perched on a hill overlooking the sparkling blue Pacific. He played thirty-six holes of golf every day, never needing more than a light sweater. Before he had to return to the January snows for which Chicago is famous, our friend applied for a California job. He was hired, starting the following month. He also put a down payment on a rather expensive home overlooking the surf, called home, and told his family to start packing. Later he ruefully remarked, "Nobody told me the weather that year was very unusual. Nobody mentioned that stretch of the coast is foggy and cold the year round. I think it was three years before we ever saw the sun again!"

Speaking of weather, even though you can't find *perfect* weather, you can surely find something much more pleasant than the weather you've had to put up with all those working years. This is one of the exciting features of retirement: For the first time in your life, work doesn't dictate where you must live, so you needn't lock yourself into one weather pattern. You can choose any climate that best fits your new lifestyle. Or, if you like, you can keep your present home and relocate to a second hometown in Arizona or Florida for a glorious winter. It takes a little gumption to get started "following the sun," but thousands upon thousands do just that, and they love it!

RETIREMENT DEVELOPMENTS

Retirees who will not be working at regular jobs have choices that are impractical for someone who has to factor in commuting distance and convenience to the workplace. One option is buying or renting in a residential development exclusively for older people, the kind with amenities such as lakes, golf courses, and swimming pools. There's often a clubhouse with a gourmet restaurant, hobby rooms, card rooms, and whatever else it takes to amuse the residents. These developments often are located miles away from town, out in the country, because the developer selects the most scenic location with the least expensive price tag for the acreage. Of course, these places would be out of the question for a family with children—unless the kiddies are over fifty years old, because that's often the minimum age.

Before you roll your eyes at the idea of an age-segregated community, thinking, "I'd rather live in town, in a mixed-age neighborhood, where we will have friends of all age groups instead of segregating ourselves with older people," you might consider this from another angle. Your younger neighbors will no doubt be nice people, friendly and helpful, but chances are you'll never become bosom buddies because you will be running on different tracks. When you want to go fishing or play golf, your neighbors have to work. If it's a weekend, there'll be a Cub Scout meeting or Little League baseball game. When you invite the parents over for a game of bridge, there will be a school function they need to attend or else they are worn out after working all day and are looking forward to kicking back and watching TV.

In a same-age community, things are different. When you move in, there'll be a social director (official or informal) who will introduce you to neighbors who have hobbies and interests that match yours. You'll

be invited to the clubhouse for bridge, dances, buffets, and other social activities. When you want to go fishing or attend a play in a nearby city, you'll find several neighbors eager to accompany you. After all, they are retired and have nothing better to do than enjoy themselves. If you'd like to take up a new hobby, such as quilting or jewelry making, there'll likely be a group in your complex that meets weekly for lessons and to share talent. A side benefit is that your lives will be more tranquil because of the absence of children and teenagers. The bottom line is that age-restricted developments offer a lifestyle in addition to real estate. With organized activities and social groups ready to welcome new residents, transition to retirement is made painless and swift. If you're not sure about any of this, many of these developments offer a "try-it-out" package—an inexpensive three-day stay while you sample the facilities, meet some of the residents, and see how it feels.

Not everyone likes these age-restricted developments. They are often more expensive than neighborhoods in town, they are isolated from the community as a whole, and they can be a long way from shopping and conveniences. Because you've most likely lived in mixed-age neighborhoods all of your lives, you could feel more comfortable living in town rather than at the lake or the golf course. If you do settle in a mixed-generation neighborhood, you may have to search to find others who do not fit the profile of young parents; they may not live next door, but surely on the next block or so.

RETIRING TO THE COUNTRY

Some potential retirees picture idyllic retirement in an isolated rural or backwoods community as being the ultimate in get-away-from-it-all living. Small crossroads villages in the Ozarks, East Texas, or Appalachia can fit the ideal of attractive, peaceful, and romantic places for retirement. A bonus of rural life is the inevitable lower cost of living, bargain housing prices, and very low crime rates.

We have mixed feelings about recommending retirement in small farming communities to folks with big-city or suburban backgrounds. Unless your family history is rooted in country tradition, you could feel very much out of place in a true country hamlet. When you share few common interests with your neighbors, it's easy to feel ignored or even ostracized. It's not that they dislike you, they just don't know what to say to you, and you have the same problem.

When almost everyone in the community is in some way involved in agriculture, everyday conversations tend to dwell on the price of soybeans or the best way to deworm hogs. When your agricultural experience is limited to watering your flower bed once a week, you may find you have few words of wisdom to share with your neighbors. When your accent sounds funny to your neighbors, and if you don't own a pickup with a cracked windshield and a defective muffler, you could be considered an oddball. People will be polite, but distant and shy. You'll receive few invitations to visit your neighbors, and you could feel very lonely. The exception to this situation is when a large number of retirees from outside the community and with similar cultural backgrounds provide a support group.

It doesn't have to be that way, of course; it depends on your personality and determination to become part of the community. We know a couple from New Jersey who fell in love with a lakeside property in the Alabama hills and bought in before they thought the situation through. Determined to "fit in," they attacked their neighbors with friendliness and insisted on participating in local affairs. By changing some of their attitudes and approaches to life, they were accepted. The husband eventually ran for election as a county supervisor and was elected.

Balance that success story with the tale of a recently divorced man who decided to retire from Philadelphia to a rustic but charming lake community in the Ozarks. His choice was based on a magazine article describing the place as one of the "top retirement towns in the U.S.A." When asked how he liked his new hometown, he shook his head and said, "As soon as my house sells, I'm outta here!" When asked why, he explained, "I was born and raised in the city. I like to sleep late in the morning and stay up late at night. At home, if I felt like a midnight snack, I could always find a restaurant open and the nearby grocery store was open 24 hours. But here, everything shuts down at eight o'clock in the evening. Everything! I even tried to learn how to fish, but I don't like to fish. I just don't fit in here." It was only after he moved to his new home that he discovered he was living in a county where no alcohol was sold. "If I want a cocktail, I need to drive 35 miles to the next county, go to a package liquor store, bring it home, and mix it myself. I hate to drink alone! This is not the place for a single man!"

His worst experience was when he received an invitation to a New Year's Eve celebration from one of the few friends he had managed to make. He was delighted to attend his first social event. The party was in the next town, about 15 miles away. He felt confident about having a few drinks because a "designated driver" volunteered to chauffeur the celebrants back home. On the way, they encountered a police roadblock. Even though the designated driver was sober, the whole lot of them were tossed into jail. The designated driver was charged with "transporting drunks" and his passengers accused of being intoxicated in public. "I just don't fit in here," the retiree repeated sadly.

The lesson is, research well before buying! The retiree could have saved a lot of time, money, and effort had he researched the move on his own and not blindly accepted someone else's statistical evaluation. Renting for a few months would have told him plenty. Even a preliminary trip to his dream town and a week in a motel could have told him almost everything he needed to know.

LOOKING FOR BARGAIN RETIREMENT LOCATIONS

When searching for an appropriate community for relocation, some retirees consider cost of living as one of the major concerns. Without question, moving to a town where homes can be purchased for one-half to one-third the cost elsewhere, or renting a home for a song, will allow a higher quality standard of living on the same income. But it's possible to place too much emphasis on low cost of living and cheap real estate as the attractions of your target community. In our travels we've encountered many places where $60,000 will buy a nice three-bedroom home, where carpenters will remodel for $9.00 per hour, where haircuts are still $6.50, and where permanent waves cost $20.00. But *inexpensive* living doesn't necessarily equate to *quality* living. It's true that some low-cost areas are exceptional bargains, offering a high-quality life with welcoming neighbors and affordable living costs. Yet other low-cost areas are intensely dreary and boring, and sometimes dangerous.

Why is the cost of living and housing dramatically less in some localities? You'll find one common explanation for cheap real estate and low rents: The town is an undesirable place to live, a town that steadily loses population because it has absolutely nothing going for it—no jobs, no charm. The area is in a permanent economic depression. Homes sell for rock-bottom prices because eager sellers outnumber reluctant buyers. Unless you are sincerely dedicated to boredom, bad weather, and cable TV, these are not places you would seek out for retirement.

There may be other reasons for unusual low costs in a town, such as an unforeseen, disastrous business slump or a trend that causes the job market to disintegrate. In this event people don't necessarily *want* to leave and seek work elsewhere. They leave because they *have* to. Homes go on the real estate market at giveaway prices because sellers have no other choice.

Although situations like this are personal tragedies for displaced families, they open windows of opportunity for retired folks. Because jobs and regular weekly paychecks aren't essential for most retired couples, quality real estate can be theirs for a fraction of what similar housing would cost elsewhere. Younger couples with children move away, making room for older people to move in. This raises the ratio between retired and working people to impressive levels. Retirees can become a majority and wield influence over local government and political processes in a way seldom found elsewhere.

We've visited several of these towns, places like the towns of Ajo and Bisbee in Arizona, where mines closed, and Colorado's Grand Junction, whose economy toppled when the shale oil industry collapsed, or Longview, Washington, where the lumber industry all but disappeared. As you might imagine, opportunities like these don't last forever. As retirees move in and snap up the bargains, prices naturally rise.

Yet they rarely rise to the level they were at before the problem occurred.

RETIREE ATTRACTION PROGRAMS

According to surveys taken by major retirement developers such as Del Webb Corporation, small-town retirement is the goal of the majority of future retirees. That is, small towns within easy driving distance of a larger city. The advantages of small-town living, besides affordable housing and inexpensive living, include the opportunity for community participation and typical small-town friendliness. The other side of the coin is that a community's economy benefits significantly with each retired couple that relocates in the community. This growing awareness of the economic and social value of retirees from outside the region is transforming the way city officials, politicians, and businesspeople think about retirees.

This awakening came about a few years ago, while town and city administrators were searching for ways to modernize and upgrade their economies. Smaller towns were particularly concerned because they were losing population as residents moved away in search of higher wages. Housing vacancies soared as home prices dropped. Retail stores were losing customers, and the tax bases were shrinking. At first the towns tried giving subsidies and tax breaks to lure industries to relocate in their communities, but they soon discovered that a factory employing low-wage workers was not the answer. The workers, without medical benefits, were forced to use emergency clinics in the local hospital, costs absorbed by taxpayers. As renters, they paid little or no property taxes, yet their children burdened the schools. And finally, with minimum-wage pay, there was little left over to spend for anything but

necessities. Soon it was apparent that subsidies and tax breaks to the new industries were a drag, not a boost, to economic development.

On the other hand, a handful of retired couples moving into the area can do wonders for the economy. They create jobs instead of taking jobs by hiring people to remodel or build new homes, spending money in retail stores, and patronizing local businesses. They have Medicare insurance and don't depend on local charity for health care. They have no children, yet they pay taxes to support the schools just the same. They are law-abiding people. Retirement experts estimate that seven retired couples moving into a community can be the economic equivalent of a factory employing dozens of minimum-wage employees.

Many small towns have given up on industrial development and instead are concentrating on attracting out-of-state retirees. They do this by creating retirement recruitment committees to reach out across the nation to welcome retirees and to encourage them to relocate. Money is being spent on both the state and community levels to lure out-of-state retirees. The idea is spreading, especially through the South, with involvement on the state as well as local levels. If you are thinking of retirement, you are on their wanted list!

Check with the chamber of commerce when researching a retirement relocation; ask whether the community has an active retiree welcoming committee or retirement attraction committee. These are hometown boosters who go out of their way to encourage out-of-state retirees to settle into their hometown.

A program typically works like this: When the committee learns that someone has made inquiries at the chamber of commerce about retirement, a volunteer gets on the telephone and invites the prospective retirees for a visit. Committee members show newcomers around the area, introduce them to other retirees, and invite them to social affairs specially designed to make newcomers feel welcome.

What does this mean to retirees? Instead of moving into an unfamiliar town as a stranger among strangers, retirees immediately enjoy a circle of welcoming friends and acquaintances. Often the committee volunteers themselves have moved in from other states and have been invited to serve on the committee. You'll have plenty of interests in common. When you request information from a chamber of commerce, no matter in what part of the country, be sure to ask if it has an active retirement committee. If there is one, you can be confident that you will be welcomed to the community as a valued friend.

WORKING DURING RETIREMENT

The concept of working after retirement used to seem out of place in a retirement plan. The retirement goal a few years ago was looking forward to the day you no longer had to wake up early every morning, gulp a cup of coffee, and hurry off to the office. Retirement was pictured as a home on the golf course or a country cottage beside a bass lake. If you simply change jobs or go into business for yourself, how can you claim to be retired?

Things have changed. Because the average age of those leaving the work-place is decreasing, through voluntary or involuntary retirement, younger, more energetic retirees adopt a different approach toward retirement, favoring early retirement and active lifestyles. Clearly, they aren't ready for a sedentary retirement lifestyle. According to surveys taken of the baby-boomer generation, most of whom have crossed the fifty-years-and-older bridge, most have plans on working at least part-time or are considering going into business. With these ideas in mind, an analysis of possible relocation communities is extremely important. Those who can do work via the Internet are lucky because they can live anywhere and still earn a paycheck. Others who plan on working as part-time consultants or possibly as vacation replacements in a company where they once worked or that does similar work will need to locate within a reasonable commuting distance. The trick is to find the most pleasant community that is near enough to commute when necessary.

On the other hand, if you don't absolutely *have* to work, why do it? If you cannot burn up your extra energy with recreational projects, and if you feel guilty about not "doing something," try volunteering. You'll feel good about yourself and you'll find your services sincerely appreciated and valued more highly than if you were to work in a fast-food restaurant or some other high-competition, low-paying job. Volunteering is also one of the easiest ways to make friends in a community. You'll find yourself rubbing shoulders with like-minded folks who share your attitudes toward life.

FINDING A NEW HOMETOWN

Armchair research is no substitute for actually traveling to your target relocation destinations and seeing things firsthand. That said, visiting all retirement possibilities would be impossible given the number of potential towns, the variety of climates, and other factors. You'll need to do nontravel research to eliminate places that don't fill your needs or meet your requirements. Your preliminary exploration is best done on the Internet and/or at your local library. Many libraries provide Internet access, and most libraries subscribe to a variety of out-of-town newspapers.

If you already have decided where you are going to relocate, you'll still be interested in what kind of place you will be calling your hometown for the next stage of your life. You probably want to do research to better understand what kind of town you will be living in and what kind of lifestyle you can expect. If you haven't yet decided exactly where you will be going, you need to research *all* towns under consideration to see which ones sound the best. Through commonsense research you can begin a process of elimination to narrow the list to a select few.

To make a final decision, you really should visit the towns under final consideration and do on-location research. Before you reach that stage, you can do a world of research without ever leaving the city limits. You can eliminate the impractical towns quickly and concentrate on the more likely candidates for relocation.

THINGS TO CONSIDER ABOUT YOUR NEW HOMETOWN

When researching a community as a possible new hometown for you and your family, consider the following factors:

• Population and traffic congestion: Some towns have not kept up with growth and have traffic clogging up streets designed for the early part of the twentieth century. Locating on the correct side of town can ease your commute. Drive around the business center during rush hour to get the feel of traffic.

• Local economy and employment: You are the only one who would have an idea about job growth and/or unemployment in your particular field or profession. But the overall economic status of a community should be easy to assess by observing the condition of the various neighborhoods and business districts. If you not looking for employment, then a sluggish economy will usually spell lower wages and prices in the region and a lower cost of living for you.

• Personal safety: The neighborhood should feel safe to you and your family. You'll need to do personal, on-location research on this.

• Location: The choice is yours; if job opportunities are plentiful around the country, you could have a wide choice of new hometowns. You can decide to live beside the ocean surf, near a mountain ski area, on the edge of a vast desert, or in a metropolitan suburb.

- Heath care: If you or a family member has special medical requirements, you'll need to know that care will be available. And, if you are retired, make sure doctors are accepting Medicare patients. If you qualify for military benefits, you might consider living near a base or a veterans' hospital.

- Education: The availability of quality schooling is important for children. A good community college can provide adult education opportunities for you and your spouse. See the College Town Relocation chapter for more information.

- Entertainment and hobbies: The new community should have similar entertainment offerings as you've been used to. If you like to go to museums, concerts, professional sports events, or the theater, your new hometown should provide these or should be within reasonable driving distance of performances.

- Outdoor and recreational activities: Each community has its own array of outdoor things to do. Make sure that your favorites are included in your new hometown or that you and your family will enjoy the new offerings if you have to give up the old activities.

- Climate: Temperature is not the only consideration. Check out the amount of rain and snow in a locality and the number of sunny days. Remember that some coastal cities have mild weather but lots of overcast, gloomy days.

- Air quality: Dirty and sooty air can cause health problems as well as be depressing. Usually these concerns are limited to the larger cities and their suburbs.

- Cost of living/tax structure: Depending on your income levels, state and local income taxes could make a difference in your budget. Property taxes vary widely between various states and even between communities within the same state. Regional costs of utilities, food, and medical care can affect your budget as well.

- Transportation: Access to an Interstate highway, intercity bus transportation, and a nearby commuter airport can be important not only for you but also for friends and family who may want to visit your new hometown.

- Access to a larger city: The most popular arrangement seems to be a small town or suburb within an easy drive of a big city. You can enjoy the friendliness and quiet ambiance of the small community yet take advantage of the city's entertainment, shopping, and professional sports events.

- Uncommon local problems: Keep an eye out for regional conditions that don't appear on the surface of your potential hometown. Mosquitoes, nearby swamps, flight paths of commercial or military aircraft, and other annoying conditions can ruin an otherwise tranquil hometown.

NEWSPAPER RESEARCH

A newspaper can be a mirror of the community, a reflection of its personality in many ways. The region's economic health, culture, belief systems, entertainment preferences, political atmosphere, and much more can be determined by reading the local newspaper. You can gain an enormous amount of knowledge about a town by thoroughly studying its news media.

Many local libraries subscribe to out-of-town newspapers—the larger the library, the wider the selection. If you live in a small town where your library doesn't provide the newspapers you want (particularly those from another state or smaller towns some distance away), write to the chamber

CLOSE-UP
Make Research a Game

Planning your move can be loads of fun for the entire family. If you don't need to decide immediately which community you will choose to be your next hometown, you have time to decide what you would like to find there when you finally arrive. Make a wish list describing your ideal location. For example, your list might look like the following:

1. No sidewalks to shovel in winter.
2. Small town not more than 45 minutes from a city.
3. No more than one-half hour drive from new job.
4. Near an interstate and an airport with commercial service.
5. Within two hours of the ocean or a large lake.
6. Local college for adult education and first two years of college for the children.
7. Plenty of hiking and biking trails.
8. A good school with athletic programs for the children (or music instruction, etc.).
9. Good medical facilities.

Then get out the maps and go to work!

of commerce in the community you are interested in and explain that you need a copy or two to make decisions about relocating there. During the course of our research on possible retirement towns, we've received many unsolicited three-month subscriptions to local newspapers simply because our contacts thought we might be prospective newcomers.

Real estate companies are also sources of hometown newspapers. If you explain that you are thinking of moving to a given town (and a potential client of the real estate office), you might receive a free three-month subscription.

A very important component of an out-of-town paper is its classified section. This gives you an in-depth view of the economy, the cost of living, and the real estate market. Compare the "help-wanted" and "work-wanted" columns and see which are longer, and look at wages asked and wages offered. Then compare these ads with the classified section of your local newspaper. This should give you an indication of what could be considered normal wages if you are thinking about part-time work, as well as what kind of competition you will have for jobs. It also tells you what you might have to pay for help around your house, or what wages are for workers. When you find handymen offering to work for $6.00 an hour compared with $17.00 an hour in your current hometown, you've learned something about the economy. Compare prices of new and used items—furniture, appliances, and automobiles—with prices listed in your local newspaper. If prices are much higher, you can figure the cost of living is also higher. Look at supermarket and national chain store advertising and compare prices with those at home. Sometimes identical specials will be priced differently; this also tells you something about the cost of living.

Check to see how crime is reported; the way a paper reports crime news tells you a lot about a town's safety. When a front-page story reports a burglary or a drunk-driving arrest, that gives you one picture. But if homicides and drive-by shootings are buried on the back pages, you have another picture, don't you?

You can also learn about a community's cultural activities from a newspaper. Announcements of plays, lectures, concerts, and community college classes open to adults tell you something about what is going on. The entertainment section may list musical groups performing at restaurants, the number of movie houses, and other popular social activities. Club activities, county fairs, and other community activities can give clues as to what is important in residents' lives. A newspaper with a section devoted to senior-citizen news indicates a high level of interest in the well-being of retirees as well as an active participation in local affairs by seniors.

Finally, because a newspaper usually reflects the political viewpoints of a community, you can determine whether your private views might make you feel uncomfortable as a nonconformist amid your new neighbors. Look at the newspaper's editorial pages to observe the publisher's political stance and see if news stories are slanted to reflect the publisher's views or if they strive for a neutral position. It's interesting how a newspaper can influence the thinking of an entire community. When a newspaper is the only source of local news, published opinions are usually accepted as fact. If you disagree with the newspaper's stance on issues, at least you will be aware of the possibility that the majority of your neighbors will feel differently than you, and you can tailor your behavior and be prepared to react accordingly. Of course, if you have strong political views, you might feel uneasy in a community where you are in a tiny minority.

Out-of-town telephone books are also found in libraries and can be a source of information. A telephone book's Yellow Pages can paint a complete picture of the town's business life. The number of banks, supermarkets, shopping centers, and other commercial entities tells you something about the vitality of business. This is where you check for bus service and taxi companies. Look at the listings under "Airlines or Airports" to see if there is a local airport and which airlines service it. A telephone book also gives an up-to-date listing for the chamber of commerce office. A letter to those groups can yield valuable information about their respective towns in the form of brochures, information on clubs and activities, lists of real estate companies, recreational opportunities, and much more.

INTERNET RESEARCH

Surely, you aren't among those who resist joining the Internet generation, are you? If so, there is still hope for you at your local library, because most libraries now provide computers for use by the public. More than

When checking out real estate, don't fail to visit "open houses." Not only will you learn about local home prices, but you may have an opportunity to meet and talk with local residents attending the open house. This is a great opportunity to hear what folks have to say about their hometown and gain some insight as to what living there will be like.

a fad, the Internet is a valuable tool for information of all conceivable kinds, and it is especially valuable for relocation research.

You can combine newspaper and Internet research when your library doesn't subscribe to the newspapers you need for your information. Many newspapers now have their own Internet Web sites. (An extensive list of U.S. newspapers can be found at newslink.org.) Internet search engines can point you to specific information about a region or town. Suppose you are looking for information about Bullhead City, Arizona. You simply go to the search engine and type in the words "Bullhead City newspaper." Within seconds an online newspaper pops up, with complete local news and a classified advertising section. You can browse the classified ads or look at real estate for sale to compare prices, as well as read about local news and community activities. You can even place your own classified ad for $1 a week, should you have an overwhelming desire to find employment in Bullhead City. (Many retirees live in Bullhead City and commute by a ferry across the Colorado River to work in the gambling casinos on the other bank, the glittering city of Laughlin, Nevada.)

Almost any town or city you might be interested in has a chamber of commerce Web page and official city Web pages that tell you about the community. You'll also find dozens of related pages packed full of information about the region, pages sponsored by local businesses, the schools, or hobby pages by individual residents. Type the name of the community into the search engine, and you will be astounded at the amount of information that comes up. You can learn about a town's history, culture, cost of living, real estate market, rentals, climate, recreational opportunities, and more.

Real estate Web pages not only list prices of properties but also often show color pictures of homes for sale. The local hospital's Web pages give you an in-depth look at local health care. You can find a weather page for your new hometown, providing daily rundowns on the temperatures and weather conditions. Larger regional industries often have Web pages that can be helpful when you are researching employment in a given community.

The amount of information available on the Internet about most communities is truly staggering. Some of it is fluff, of course; every community wants to put its best foot forward. But the hard facts and details are there for you to absorb. Many pages have e-mail addresses inviting you to ask questions. Real estate companies always have e-mail addresses that you can use to ask detailed questions.

CHAMBER OF COMMERCE

A community's chamber of commerce is another important contact point for relocation research. You can make contact in person, by e-mail, or by regular mail. An inquiry about relocating in the community should unleash a flood of brochures and letters from real estate professionals, banks, and others who see you as a potential client should you decide to move into town. Some offices charge for sending information. To be fair, the more popular places find this quite an expense to mail hundreds of packets a week.

Most chamber offices are eager to help you relocate and will do just about anything to help you get settled and to convince you that living in their town is next to paradise. But don't be surprised if the person behind the counter isn't the least bit interested in your idea of relocating in their town. Some chamber of commerce offices are staffed by minimum-wage employees who seem to resent folks coming in to ask questions and interfering with their reading. When this is the case, you might ask for an interview with the chamber manager and ask him or her for some inside recommendations about relocating in town. The best chamber of commerce personnel are volunteers who have relocated to this town themselves; they can be of enormous help.

REAL ESTATE AGENCIES

Real estate agencies can be valuable sources of information about relocation. Brokers and sales staff know the neighborhoods, all there is to know about schools, and what businesses in town are likely to be hiring new personnel. This is their business! Once you make contact with an office, you will find them clinging to your elbow, making suggestions for properties, doing everything they can to convince you to relocate to their town. If you hint that you'd like to see a copy or two of the local newspaper, you'll probably have a package heading your way in the next mail. Sometimes they'll actually give you a short subscription to the newspaper. Even if you decide not to buy, a real estate professional will know what is for rent and can usually set you up with a place to stay while you look around at homes for sale.

USE YOUR CONNECTIONS

Is it possible that you have social, fraternal, or church connections between your community and your possible new hometown? If you belong to a public service, business, or fraternal organization, such as Rotary Club, Toastmasters, Lions, Masons, Knights of Columbus, VFW, Elks, Moose, or similar organizations, you may find great connections for research. Who would better know about employment opportunities in a community? Who would be more likely to welcome you or to advise you about schools,

doctors, the preferred neighborhoods, and so forth? When you visit your prospective town, be sure to attend the church service and go to the "coffee hour" afterward and chat with people. Ask questions. Once people know of your interest in their community, they will be most eager to help you. You will not only learn the good and bad about the town but also lay the foundation for a circle of friends later on.

VISIT YOUR FINAL CANDIDATES

You can gather only so much information about a faraway place from your neighborhood library and your home office. Once you've done your homework, you'll need to make an on-the-spot inspection of your potential hometown. An in-person visit allows you and your family to stroll through the downtown section, tour the neighborhoods, smell the flowers, sample the restaurants, and pretend you already live here. Part of how we evaluate a town is to imagine we live there and think about how it feels. Sensations and feelings such as this cannot be quantified or ranked from one to twenty. You'll not find these feelings on the Internet or in chamber of commerce brochures. What you may remember most from your visit could be the way people nodded and said, "Good morning," as they passed by, or how the mountains hovering over the town made you feel refreshed. Your visit is not just to check out the local cost of living but also how you feel as you sip a drink while looking out over a deep blue lake at dusk.

The more times you can visit, the better. If you can find an apartment complex where you can rent by the week, you'll learn even more about the town: how shopping is, whether traffic gets snarled up during rush hours, and what the place is like on weekends. The time of year and season could influence you unfairly. Beautiful summer weather is nice, but when sub-zero winds whip through the streets in the winter, you may not think it's so beautiful.

USING YOUR RV FOR RESEARCH

There is no better way to learn about a community than actually living there, even for a short time. You'll experience how the town feels, learn about the kind of people who live there, compare the cost of living, and savor the community's general ambiance. If you are the owner of an RV, now is the time to haul it out of storage and put it to work doing research for your new hometown. Travel to several of your candidate communities and try each one on for size, even if only for a few days. Obviously, viewing a community from a motel room is much different from having your own place (albeit an aluminum box on wheels), doing your shopping at the local supermarkets, and visiting the downtown area for lunch. And it's not very expensive. Whereas a nice motel can cost $60 to $90 a night in most areas, an RV park might charge $15 to $25. For longer stays, you can often find a park for $250 or $300 a month. The bonus is that you and your family needn't run up large restaurant bills; you brought your kitchen and dining room with you.

Those who are looking over the job situation in a town can learn a lot by visiting facilities of prospective employers. You can look over the plant and offices, perhaps speak with employees, and possibly gain some insight as to whether this might be a good move for your career. This can all be achieved before you actually make the appointment to present your résumé to the personnel department. You can also check out other businesses with the possibility of locating a job with competing companies.

If your target town is one of your seasonal vacation favorites, there's a possibil-

Make a point of visiting the commercial center at rush hour to see how congested traffic can be at its worst-case scenario. Study the traffic patterns between your possible new home and where you will be working. You could save many hours of commute time depending on which side of town you choose to live.

ity that you might catch a temporary job to help cover expenses while you are testing the waters of your future hometown. It turns out that there is a large subculture of "snowbirds" who regularly tour the country in their RVs, working temporary, seasonal jobs. The pay is often far from generous, but free RV parking and utilities are usually part of the benefits package. Employers are continually in need of temporary workers during the tourist season and are happy to find help.

An excellent publication, *Workamper News,* brings workers and employers together with page after page of temporary and permanent "help-wanted" ads. Although the paper was originally directed toward RV owners (and still is to a large extent), the publication lists jobs of all descriptions for people with or without their own housing. The publishers try to weed out phony get-rich-quick schemes, so most of the help-wanted ads are legitimate. Each listing includes information on the job location, duties, benefits, and how and where to apply. Visit the Web site www.workamper.com for more information.

RESEARCHING PERSONAL SAFETY

When casting about for a new hometown, one of your priorities should be a neighborhood in which you and your family can feel secure. A few years ago we bought a

Crime Prevention Tips

Your local office on aging and the police department can help you make your home or apartment more secure. In most communities these organizations sponsor crime prevention projects and work together to publish educational materials about crime prevention.

Often your police department will be happy to make a free "burglary audit" of your home. A police officer will come to your home to check on your home security and make suggestions for your safety. Some of the more common security recommendations include the following:

1. Always lock your garage, even if you are at home or are just stepping out briefly.
2. When you are out of the house, lock your windows as well as your doors.
3. Cut back bushes near doors and windows.
4. Install dead-bolt locks and night chains.
5. Install and use a peephole in your door.
6. Keep outside areas well illuminated.
7. Keep valuable personal property in a safe-deposit box rather than at home.
8. Do not keep large amounts of cash in the house.
9. Do not hide an extra set of keys to your home in obvious places, such as under the doormat, on the ledge above your door, in a planter box, or in the mailbox.

If you go away on a trip:

1. Use timers to keep lights on inside and outside the house in the evening.
2. Stop mail and newspaper deliveries and ask a neighbor to pick up circulars and packages from your driveway.
3. Hide your empty garbage cans.
4. Arrange for someone to maintain your yard.
5. Turn your telephone bell down.

summer home in a small Oregon community (population less than 100). When we inquired about safety there, we learned that most residents never locked their cars, and some even left the keys in the ignition so they wouldn't lose them! On the other hand, friends living in a nearby city didn't lock their cars, either, but for a different reason. Automobile break-ins were so common in their neighborhood that locking a car was an invitation for a thief to break a window to see what valuable prize might

be locked inside. Yet in the better neighborhoods of that same city, people felt perfectly safe.

Obviously, the larger the city, the larger the potential for crime. But that's like saying that the larger the city, the larger number of delivery trucks on the streets and the more traffic accidents caused by delivery trucks. It all depends upon the neighborhood. Yes, you will find much higher crime rates in large metropolitan areas such as Los Angeles or Washington, D.C., than in Walla Walla, Washington, or Resume Speed, Arkansas. But official crime statistics don't tell the whole story.

Curiously, in some large-city neighborhoods—not so very far away from high-crime areas—people can leave their doors unlocked and can walk home from a late movie without anxiety. For example, Hermosa Beach, an affluent suburb in the Los Angeles metropolitan area, ranks exceptionally high in safety even though it's just twenty minutes away from one of the most crime-ridden areas in Los Angeles.

The California town where we live has one of the lowest murder rates in the country, averaging one murder every three or four years. A sister city a half-hour drive away has a gang problem, several shootings a week, and at least two or three murders a month. Yet this city recently received an award from a national magazine as one of the "most livable retirement cities" in the nation. To be fair, the shootings take place in neighborhoods far away from where retirees buy their homes, and many people who live there feel perfectly safe.

Every year the FBI publishes an extensive, in-depth report on crime in the United States. Called the *Uniform Crime Report,* the book contains many tables listing, among other things, crime statistics for U.S. towns with populations of 10,000 and up. Every possible crime from murder to shoplifting makes the reports and are transmitted to the FBI archives. As in-depth as this study is, the FBI warns against using the statistics to rate communities regarding personal safety. There are several problems with the statistics, partly because of the way the individual police departments report crime. Some report the theft of comic books or motorists driving away from a gas station without paying, while others don't report anything but serious felonies. Some police departments

don't mention crimes like rape and arson in their reports. Another statistical error is reporting by police in tourist locations, where during the popular seasons the number of people in town can double or triple the permanent resident population, yet the crimes get prorated using the smaller, official population. This presents an unfair picture of crime in the resort town. Finally, the FBI statistics include crimes that do not directly affect the personal safety of those living in the community. For example, shoplifting from a merchant or theft from a coin machine is of much less concern to you and your neighbors than burglaries or muggings.

After years of struggling with crime statistics, we've come to the conclusion that you must do your own personal safety research based on your personal observations. Earlier we mentioned using the local newspaper as a research tool and how the general crime climate can be deduced from the news articles. This is especially true of smaller cities and towns. The lesson is this: When murders and rapes are reported on page 23, if at all, you can assume that violent crime is a problem. On the other hand, if a burglary makes the front page, then burglaries can't be all that common. Newspapers in smaller cities often publish a detailed police log. Read it over carefully and see what is considered to be serious crime in this town. When police are involved in cases such as rescuing a cat from Mrs. Smith's tree or recovering a bicycle stolen from Jimmy Jones's front yard, you can be sure that crime isn't exactly out of control.

That said, in tourist-oriented communities, the weekly police log can be deceiving. A friend who is a police officer in a prime tourist area complains that serious crimes are often concealed from the local newspaper. The police chief and city officials want to present a calm and peaceful front so as not to scare away tourists or potential buyers of resort property. In other words, read between the lines if it's a tourist-oriented area you are considering. Conversing with residents can tell you a lot about personal safety in any community.

INVESTIGATE ON YOUR OWN

You can tell a lot about a community's safety factor by driving and strolling through the neighborhoods. Are the homes neat, with trimmed shrubbery and mowed lawns? Or are they shabby, obviously owned by absentee landlords? Are there old junkers parked around the neighborhood? Stop and talk with people working in their yards, walking their dogs, or shopping in the corner market. Let them know you are considering a relocation move and they'll be happy to share their knowledge. If folks feel safe living there, they're happy to tell you all about it. If they suggest getting a weapon to protect yourself, it's probably not a safe neighborhood.

Real estate people can help you here. Try to find a neighborhood with older, mature residents; your chances for peace are better there. You can often judge the safety of an area by its general affluence. It turns out that the wealthiest neighborhoods in an area are usually by far the safest, with exceptionally low rates of burglary, larceny, and robbery. This is true for several reasons. First of all, law enforcement in upscale neighborhoods tends to be more efficient than in poor neighborhoods. Also, these locations tend to have fewer teenagers in residence—again, the presence of unsupervised youngsters is directly related to the burglary rate. And, finally, strangers with criminal intentions tend to stand out in wealthy neighborhoods and get reported to police before the strangers get a chance to commit a crime.

While large cities usually have safe and comfortable neighborhoods, most small towns definitely offer a much safer feeling. On the other hand, just because a town seems peaceful doesn't make it a great place to live. It could also be so boring that burglars and robbers can't stand working there, or perhaps it's so cold in the wintertime that car thieves can't get the cars started. But that is another issue.

HOUSING OPTIONS

When relocating to a new community, you may find yourself a bit unsure as to whether or not you are making the correct choice. Try as you might to research your best, sometimes, hidden beneath the smooth surface of an otherwise lovely community, you could find some rocky conditions in your new hometown that just are not the best for you and your family. The new job you counted on turns out to be somewhat unpleasant or not a permanent position after all. Your children discover that the schools where you purchased your new home are the worst in the district, and the kids hate the teachers. Your commute to work takes forever over traffic-clogged highways and could have been a snap had you purchased your home on the other side of town. Problems such as these are discouraging and difficult to overcome once you have sunk all the equity from the sale of your previous home into your new place. You stand to lose plenty if forced to sell.

One solution, aside from doing better research on your new hometown in the first place, is to consider some alternative housing situations. When you relocate voluntarily, you have more options for housing, and you might want to experiment with renting a house or trying alternative housing before you buy that new home on the golf course. Instead of buying a home right away, you might find that temporary quarters will do perfectly well while you learn about the town. In most communities house, apartment, and condo rentals are plentiful. But in smaller towns you'll often find that apartments and condos are scarce to nonexistent; single family homes with large yards are the norm there.

WHY NOT RENT?

It makes sense to try out a community by renting a house or apartment until everyone in the family is convinced that this relocation is going to succeed. It could take several months to be sure your new job is just what you want, for your children to decide if the school district is ideal, and for you to thoroughly investigate all possible neighborhoods for the exact house you have been dreaming about. In the meantime, a comfortable, convenient rental could be the best way to go. You needn't worry about maintenance, insurance, or utilities, and the landlord often maintains the landscaping. Should you find that you enjoy living in your temporary home, you might consider renting as a permanent

---

An excellent way to scope out a town and see if you will enjoy living there is to find a short-term apartment rental. This gives you a chance to check out the shopping and learn which part of town is best for permanent digs.

Living "Rent-Free"

One common belief is that when your home is paid for, you will be living rent-free. While it is comforting to own your home outright, you cannot realistically figure that you'll be living there for free. Look at it this way: A business considers its store, office, or factory as a capital investment; your home is exactly the same type of investment. Let's suppose your home is worth $150,000. That's your capital investment. Even with a fluctuating stock market, it's always possible to find safe investments paying good interest, say 5 to 6 percent. This means the capital investment you have in your home's equity could be returning $9,000 a year, or about $750 a month. Add to that amount taxes, insurance, and upkeep—probably another $2,500 a year. This brings the cost of living in a "rent-free" home to $958 a month. In many communities $958 could pay the rent on a home worth $150,000, and you would have $150,000 capital at your disposal should you need it.

arrangement, avoiding the responsibilities and large investment in home ownership.

For many people the mere thought of not owning their own home is blasphemy. The ideal goal for many is to eventually have a home paid for, so the family can live "rent-free." When relocating to another community, one of the first things on their agenda is to buy a new house, transferring the equity from the old home into the new mortgage. On the other hand, it could be that the income from investing that money into long-term bonds or some other interest-paying fund could cover the rent on your home, and you would still have your capital free when you need it.

Let's examine some common beliefs about home ownership and see if they're still valid, given your present relocation agenda. Your age can be an important factor here. Home ownership, even though monthly payments are high, clearly makes sense for a young couple whose earning power probably will grow over the years. As time goes by, they pay off the loan with larger paychecks; they are building for the future. But if you are older or are consider-

ing retirement, you might want to consider whether it wouldn't be better to invest your money in your upcoming retirement rather than in some nebulous future thirty years down the line. Will you be able to enjoy your money as much thirty years from now as you can today? How old will you be then? Figure out the financial advantages for yourself realistically, with an eye on today, not thirty years in the future.

RENTING PERMANENTLY VERSUS BUYING

The issue of permanently renting your home versus buying is not easily resolved. Property values vary so widely from one community to another, and appreciation of the home is different. The monthly costs of renting are usually lower than buying, but you need to consider inflation, property costs, and appreciation. If property seems to be appreciating at a higher rate than inflation, then buying could be a better long-term deal.

Much depends on the property value and the rents being charged. For example, suppose $150,000 is an average price for a three-bedroom home in an average neighborhood; such a home would rent for an average of $970 a month. Purchasing a $150,000 home with a $15,000 down payment and a thirty-year, 8 percent mortgage results in a monthly payment of $1,028 a month. Add taxes, insurance, and so forth to bring the monthly outlay to $1,228. Obviously, it would be less expensive to rent for the short term.

The key here is your take on the future: If you believe that the rate of appreciation in the value of your home will continue to rise as it has in the past ten years, buying might be a better long-term strategy, especially if you are convinced that you and your family will be happy here for the next twenty years. Sometimes rents will be higher than average, so if the monthly costs of buying are basically the same as renting, then you should think about buying. But if you believe real estate is currently at a market peak and the economy is about to go into a recession, it could be better to rent and let property values and rents fall. If you believe that we are currently at the bottom of the market and the economy will be getting dramatically better, then it could be better to buy than rent.

In a place like San Francisco, the same house could cost $600,000 and rent for $2,063 a month. Not many people can afford to buy at these rates, so renting seems to be the obvious solution. If you can swing a $600,000 home, then it will depend on your confidence in the future of inflation and appreciation.

What are some disadvantages of renting? For someone who's always owned a home, there's a vague feeling of insecurity. If you're renting a house, you never know if the owner is going to put it on the market, forcing you to move. When you are younger, moving is no big deal; but as you grow older, the chore looms larger and

Both appreciation and inflation do well for a homeowner's future equity. Appreciation increases the value of the house, while inflation lowers the value of dollars needed to pay off the loan. Over the years, they've usually worked hand-in-hand, making homes bought thirty years ago worth big money. There's no guarantee, however, that this will continue in the future.

more distasteful. The bottom line is undeniable: You lose the sense of security that comes with home ownership. Also, property ownership is a valuable hedge against inflation. Should the economy go into an inflationary spiral as it did in the 1970s, property values will climb and your equity will increase accordingly. A crystal ball and the advice of an investment counselor might be useful here.

MOBILE HOMES

For those without children, an inexpensive mobile home community can be an efficient way of owning a home, even if on a temporary basis. By using some of the equity from the sale of your last home to purchase a used, not-too-expensive mobile home, you'll have a home base that should be relatively easy to resell should you decide that relocating here was a mistake. Remember that brand-new mobile homes have a devastating rate of depreciation—even worse than new cars—so do not get caught with something you might have to sell for a loss!

A word of caution about buying a mobile home: Make sure you do not go overboard and buy something you cannot afford. Our recommendation is, do not buy anything unless you can afford to pay cash, and buy from a private party, not from a dealer or broker. The commission added to the price can be trouble. The kinds of mobile homes we recommend run between $15,000 and $40,000 in a nice park, whereas a new unit of the same size can cost $65,000 to $100,000. Interest rates on mobile home loans are much higher than conventional loans, and loans are made for a much shorter period of time. The combined payments (with high interest) and park rent can be double the rent for a really nice house. (With a rental home, you don't tie up any of your own money.) Throughout the country, many mobile homes sit empty, repossessed after their owners couldn't afford to make payments. A simple classified ad in the newspaper is usually enough to sell if you bought it for a fair price in the first place. Conventional homes take a lot more time to sell, and you will have to pay a hefty commission to the real estate agent.

Mobile-home living can be an often misunderstood mode of life. There's a lingering reputation from the early days, when "house trailers" were considered suitable for vagabonds. The presence of run-down, dreary trailer parks on the edge of many cities gives more conventional modes of mobile-home living an undeservedly poor reputation.

Today's mobile-home parks can be as upscale as you can afford. Some have adults-only policies and cater to middle-class, often affluent retirees. Facilities are tailored to couples or singles who want exceptional personal safety, friendly neighbors, and a club-like atmosphere. This lifestyle attracts a great number of people who could afford more expensive housing but who prefer to place their home sale profits into income-producing investments. In some parts of the country, such as Florida, Arizona, and California, the luxury levels of mobile-home parks can be

astounding. Often they incorporate such features as an eighteen-hole golf course, a lake, Olympic-size swimming pool, and a clubhouse worthy of a country club.

Modern-day mobile homes have nothing in common with the small, cramped house trailers found in the older parks in the poor neighborhoods of the community. The standard width of a mobile home today is 12 feet, with lengths up to 70 feet. Generally, two of these units are joined together to form a doublewide, providing a large, two-bedroom home. If you've ever visited one of the expensively furnished display models at a mobile-home sales lot, you've probably been dazzled by the luxury and spaciousness.

Many benefits accrue to this lifestyle besides low-cost, carefree living, not the least of which are friendly neighbors and social activities. The better parks have a large recreation and social hall, usually next to the swimming pool, where dinners, club meetings, bingo, and dances are regular activities. Some luxury parks offer amenities such as swimming pools, hot tubs, Jacuzzis, tennis courts, spacious clubhouses, and just about everything you'd expect to find in expensive apartment and luxury condo complexes. You don't have to worry about landscaping or maintenance of anything but your own small plot of ground. Even individual landscaping chores are sometimes taken care of by the park management. And because mobile-home communities are enclosed by fences and have limited outside access, they can be exceptionally safe places to live. Some of the more expensive places have security guards posted at the entrances around the clock. In any case, because the homes are close together and because residents know one another far better than in traditional neighborhoods, criminal activities usually are quickly noted.

Mobile homes can be perfect for those approaching retirement with the idea of selling their home and "drawing in their horns" by buying a mobile home. Many consider this an ideal way to live in comfort, convenience, and on a minimal amount of money. Approximately five million mobile homes in the United States house millions of people. In the Carolinas, about 20 percent of the housing is mobile homes, so this lifestyle is nothing new.

Many of the better parks are exclusively inhabited by retirees. Those who choose the mobile-home lifestyle point out that this is one option for home ownership without the high investment and real estate taxes that go with conventional property. As one couple said, "It costs us only $200 a month to live in our own home. And that includes water, garbage, and sewer. We don't pay property taxes; instead, we buy a license plate." Not all mobile-home parks are inexpensive, of course; some charge as much as or more than apartment rentals in the same neighborhood. In most communities you have a wide range of costs and luxuries from which to choose.

Many rural localities allow mobile homes on private property as alternative housing. This is an excellent option when you need living quarters while building that home on your view lot by the lake.

Much of a mobile home's value depends on the quality of the park in which it is located. To maintain quality standards, many mobile home parks will not accept older units. When a mobile home becomes fifteen years old or more, some parks will insist that when sold, it must be removed from the park. Be careful about investing in a mobile home that cannot be sold later.

Because mobile homes come complete with kitchen and bathroom plumbing, stove, and refrigerator, as well as most furnishings, all you need to do is find a level place to park, hook up to a sewer, or install a septic tank, and you have instant housing, comfortable and convenient. Once the new house is finished, you can sell the mobile home with a classified advertisement in the local newspaper.

This arrangement can be permanent, of course. As you drive through the typical countryside, you'll often see acreage with horse pastures, small farming plots, and barns, with a large mobile home for the main house. When installed properly—with imaginative landscaping and fencing—a mobile home can be mistaken for a conventional structure.

SETTLING INTO THE COMMUNITY

When you leave your home, friends, and perhaps family to relocate in a new community, you have some fundamental social adjustments to make. If you don't reestablish a network of friends and acquaintances and become involved in the community around you, you could feel homesick and regret leaving your old hometown. This can be especially true when the community's cultural setting and personality are foreign to you. If, for example, you and your family are city people and you find yourself in a rural, agricultural setting, you could feel ignored and isolated. The reverse could be true: You could be from a small town and find yourself in a totally different world, where neighbors talk funny and have unique and puzzling cultural values. It's usually better not to experiment with culture shock, but occasionally it's unavoidable because a career move takes you to this setting or because this town has everything else going for it. The way to avoid homesickness and isolation is to work at becoming involved with the community, to make yourself known in subtle ways, and to begin collecting a new circle of friends.

Those who are moving because of a company-sponsored relocation will have a much easier job of settling into their new community and making friends than those who drop in cold turkey. When the "sponsored-move" families arrive, they probably will be welcomed by coworkers who graciously usher them into the local society and introduce them to friends and neighbors. The newcomers will receive invitations to dinner and other social events. Within days the work-related friends may be inviting them to participate in community affairs. When the newcomers begin the new job, their circle of acquaintances and friends will increase like ripples on a pond. Should your new community be a hopeless cultural wasteland, it won't seem so hopeless because your coworkers will provide a common milieu for social integration with friends of your own social and cultural level.

STARTING OVER WITH NEW FRIENDS

Those who relocate on their own have to start from scratch. They have no one to greet them. They need strategies for making friends and influencing people in the new community so they don't feel as strangers in a strange land.

Unless this is an unusual community, do not expect folks to overwhelm you with friendliness when you first move into the neighborhood. Realize that too much friendliness on your part, at least at first, can turn your neighbors off. They already have a circle of friends, and you are an unknown quantity. Our strategy is to introduce ourselves briefly to our neighbors, explaining who we are and why we have moved into the neighborhood, and then graciously withdraw to avoid seeming "pushy," anticipating moves of sociability on the part of our new neighbors. Asking for advice or recommendations for shopping or other information about the community helps break the ice. Even really stuck-up and resentful people are flattered by this; asking for help gives them an opportunity to demonstrate their knowledge and superiority. Unless you picked a really "closed-shop" neighborhood, you will soon be making acquaintances.

Prepare yourselves to find interests in common with your new neighbors. Read the local newspaper from front to back to see what concerns residents have, and what might be topics of conversation. Remember that the local newspaper can be a weather vane of public opinion; the newspaper's editorial policy—and the way it reports the news—can be surprising influential in shaping public opinion in the first place. Watch the local TV evening news show to learn more about local personalities, gossip, and whatever is going on so that you can talk sensibly and feel like "one of the crowd." Even if you hate sports, be aware of how the high school basketball or football teams are doing and what their chances are of winning. The rule is: Do not criticize local conditions or get into political discussions until you know exactly which way the wind blows. The biggest complaint that Oregonians have about Californians who relocate in their midst is that they keep saying, "Well, in *California*, we do things differently!" Keeping quiet may be hard to do, but you should have investigated the politics before you moved here. Now is the time to keep your mouth shut—for a while, anyway.

SELECTIVE FRIENDSHIPS

Keeping quiet can be a tremendous bore, and, depending upon your personality and political views, difficult to pull off. The good news is that most of your new friends will not necessarily include your immediate neighbors. Unless you have stumbled into a really, *really* far-out community, you'll quickly gravitate to your own kind of people.

How to find your soul mates? Go where they hang out, and become a joiner. If you have children, join the PTA, get involved with recreational groups, and volunteer for school activities. If you play bridge, join the local duplicate or social bridge club. If you don't play bridge, this is a good time to learn how. Why? Because it turns out that bridge players are usually the old-time, solid members of the town's social set and can be your introduction to various social circles. The American Contract Bridge League has a national campaign to bring in new members throughout the country (it's worried that younger people aren't learning the game) and have instituted a program known as "Easy Bridge," with low-cost lessons. The local bridge players welcome newcomers with enthusiasm, knowing that they will be the bridge partners of tomorrow.

If you play golf, the country club is a great place to belong. More important than just playing golf and tennis, you'll be invited to dinners, dances, card parties, and a continuous stream of social activities. Often there are programs for members' children. In some parts of the country, particularly in southern states, the local country club may be the only place in the county with a first-class restaurant where you can legally have a cocktail at the bar and a bottle of wine served with your dinner. If you can possibly afford it, by all means join the country club!

DIFFERENT STRATEGIES

Another way to meet kindred spirits is through adult education. Most communities have a range of continuing education programs offered through local colleges or high schools, with evening classes that let you take noncredit classes in those interesting subjects you've always wanted to study. Tuition is affordable, sometimes free for adults, with no tests or grades involved. You can take classes in anything that feeds your interests, including courses covering such topics as Chinese cooking, trout fly tying, conversational Spanish, computer basics, short-story writing, or any of the fascinating classes offered in most school districts. These not only are fun but you'll also find yourself in contact with kindred spirits who share your interests.

If you have some special skills or knowledge of a subject, you might volunteer to teach a class at the local community college. Once, when we relocated into the town of Grants Pass, Oregon, I offered to conduct a seminar called "Marketing your Freelance Articles." It was a great experience because it introduced dozens of would-be writers to one another and fostered camaraderie, resulting in the formation of some self-help groups. In the process I made several good friends. When I offered to teach another class later on, they talked me into teaching a conversational Spanish class instead. My wife agreed to help me as an assistant, and we met a new group of local residents for whom travel to Spain or Mexico were interests in common. We were invited to join a fiction writers' monthly workshop, where we made several friendships that have endured to this day, long after we pulled up stakes in Oregon and moved on.

An excellent way to jump into community affairs is through volunteer activities. Plenty of opportunity exists in almost all communities. Volunteering at the local seniors' center, for Meals on Wheels, or RSVP (the Retired and Senior Volunteer Program)

Don't assume that those golf course communities are exclusively for golfers. Statistics show that in some localities, fewer than 50 percent of the residents actually play golf. Many choose to live there because of the plush surroundings and the secure feeling of a gated community. The clubhouse is the community social center, with dinners, dances, and other regularly scheduled events.

is an interesting way to meet other volunteers while doing something that makes you feel good. If you are retired, volunteering has another benefit: You will become well known among other retiree volunteers. Someday down the road, when you yourself may be in need of volunteer help, you can be sure you will be on the top of the list for friends to help you.

Volunteering at the local chamber of commerce gives you the opportunity to meet the town's "movers and shakers" and to get on a first-name basis with them as they wander in and out of the chamber office for meetings and appointments with others. Businesspeople and activists often use the chamber's offices as an unofficial city hall. Being at the front desk also places you in a position of meeting and greeting others who are investigating the community as *their* relocation choice. This gives you the chance to select friends before they actually relocate into the community. We once interviewed a couple who had moved to a small city in Utah because of a magazine article that described the place as one of the "Top Twenty Retirement Towns" in the country. They fell in love with an affordable home in a lovely neighborhood and arranged financing several months before retirement. But when they relocated, they discovered that every one of the families in their neighborhood was Mormon, and the custom was to associate mainly with other Mormons. They were invited to join the church, but declined. They found the chamber of commerce not only a social outlet but also a way to make friends with others in the community who were also in the minority and also looking to enlarge their circle of sociable friends.

This brings up another point about "outsiders" meeting resistance from long-time residents, particularly in certain regions of the country. Once we were researching a lovely Appalachian community, rather isolated in the mountain glades but popular with out-of-state summer-season residents as well as a growing number of retirees. We asked the chamber of commerce director how out-of-state newcomers were welcomed into the community. She thought about this for a moment before replying. "Well, we tend to be friendly to everyone, but it's the *outsiders* who are most friendly to other outsiders." She added, "Outsiders have to learn to accept mountain people for who we are: sincere, hard-working folks who enjoy a simple life. We hate it when outsiders try to change things." The lesson here might be, if you can't join the locals, then band together with your fellow expatriates.

GATED DEVELOPMENTS

Relocating into a gated development, often with a golf course and country club–type community center, takes much of the work out of meeting people and finding common interests. Residents have a mutual interest in welcoming you, because you are, after all, part of the infrastructure now. Often there is an official (or unofficial) social director who lists the social and recreational programs on the menu and makes sure you are introduced to the appropriate companions. You will be matched with golf partners, those who share your hobbies, and be on the guest list for special dinners and dances. These developments can be more expensive (not always), but you could save a lot of time and energy by meeting people with similar interests.

CHURCHES AND SOCIAL STRUCTURE

Depending upon the region in which you relocate, church membership can make a huge difference in your acceptance into the community. A very close friend of mine was once married to a junior executive for a chemical corporation who was transferred every two years from one station to another. She said the first thing they would do after settling into their new abode would be to attend a Sunday service in the nearest Episcopal church. After the service the priest always introduces new couples or visitors to the members of the congregation and urges everyone to welcome the newcomers. Before the afternoon was over, they would have some sincere invitations from families to come to dinner, join in social activities, or place their children in the church's day care program.

In most sections of the United States, churches and religion play a minor role in most people's lives. In many communities the majority of the population attends church sporadically; an estimated 28 million American adults *never* go to church.

There are some regions where this is not the case, where missing a Sunday service requires a valid excuse. Never to attend is looked upon as a personal flaw. This is particularly true of many communities in the South, where attending church on Sunday is as much a part of the weekly routine as mowing the lawn. Close friends almost always belong to the same church. This is sometimes difficult to understand for folks moving in from regions where churches are considered more casually, but it's important to understand how the social system works.

Some newcomers have a problem with this; they refuse to conform just for the sake of appearances. However, showing up at a church once in a while can make relocation easier. The moment strangers show up, churchgoers begin shaking hands, inquiring where they are from, and welcoming the newcomers to their new hometown. We've interviewed numerous retirees who relocated to the South from northern states and who seldom, if ever, attended church where they came from but are now members of a congregation.

FAVORITE RETIREMENT LOCATIONS

Over the years we've seen remarkable changes in the way folks view retirement and in the lifestyles they choose after leaving the job market. Not too long ago, most people couldn't conceive of retiring before they were forced to do so. They stubbornly stayed at their jobs until age sixty-five and even longer. When they finally took their retirement—often forced to quit because of health or because employers wanted a younger workforce—the concept of moving away from their homes and creating a new lifestyle for their senior years often didn't occur to them. Retirement meant staying home, working in the garden, and taking yearly vacations to Florida much the same as they had done all their working lives. The more adventurous actually moved to Florida or California, but most stayed home to tend the garden and watch TV.

Suddenly retirement concepts shifted. This was partly because of the improved financial condition of the average retiree, but mostly because of the worldview of those approaching retirement in the mid-1980s. Before that time, the average retiree had begun his working career during the Depression, a time when jobs were scarce and extremely valuable possessions. Surrendering a perfectly good job before one was forced to do so was unthinkable.

Today's retirees generally enjoyed better working conditions and higher salaries. They tend to view work in a different way than did the previous generation. A job isn't sacred or irreplaceable—leisure time is just as important as a job! This younger generation enjoys taking long vacations whenever possible and visualizes retirement as one long vacation, lasting the rest of their lives.

These new concepts have given rise to totally new retirement lifestyles. For one thing, moving away from the old hometown is a more common goal as younger people see unlimited possibilities for new beginnings. Florida and California aren't necessarily included in these possibilities. This generation isn't at all interested in the quiet, sedentary retirement of their parents. Gardening is not at the top of the agenda. Instead, they think in terms of skiing, deep-sea fishing, and outdoor recreation of all descriptions. This new wave of retirees also is better educated than their parents; college was much too expensive for most who grew up during the Depression. The new retirees fondly remember their days at the university and long to recreate that nostalgia by retiring in college towns, enjoying the cultural atmosphere, and joining other retirees in taking enjoyable classes in subjects they might have wanted to study during their college years but didn't have the time for.

One final observation: A large percentage of those retirees who move away for retirement really have no intention of *totally* retiring. They are too young and full of energy to simply stop going. One of the trends in retirement relocation is choosing smaller communities that offer part-time employment opportunities in the retiree's field or small towns within reasonable commuting distance of a larger city for part-time jobs or consulting positions. Self-employment is another popular option, whether working via the Internet or starting or buying a business.

The bottom line is that relocation for retirement is a totally different ballgame from moving for career purposes. You have an exceptionally wide choice of places and lifestyles, choices that you can tailor to your own particular needs and desires. Below is a partial list of places we've investigated and that we can recommend for retirement relocation. Most will not be appropriate for everyone, so you'll have to do your own research and make your own decisions.

Think your options through carefully, taking into consideration items such as whether your new hometown will be a place where your children and friends will want to visit, whether you will feel like a stranger from a different part of the country, and whether there might be part-time employment if you need it. You will note a definite bias in our selections, favoring warmer environments. Most retirees, when considering relocation, think in terms of places where ice and snow do not figure prominently. We agree, convinced that retirement in a climate that requires hibernating in a warm house over long periods of freezing weather is not conducive to good health.

APPALACHIAN VIRGINIA AND WEST VIRGINIA

In our ongoing search for places where quality retirement lifestyles can be enjoyed on ordinary budgets and where nice homes sell at affordable prices, we occasionally encounter a "sleeper." Our latest discovery is a beautiful Appalachian locale straddling the border between Virginia and West Virginia. Four towns—two on the Virginia side, two on the West Virginia side—joined forces to lure retirees into their communities to replace residents who moved away because of an economic slump. They describe their region as "Four Seasons Country." The cost of living here is among the lowest in the country, and quality housing is going for a song—truly a buyer's market.

This is an Appalachian wonderland, with mountains, rivers, and forests as a background. The towns are full of friendly residents who will welcome you as new neighbors. The climate lives up to its four-seasons nickname, the region being blessed with glorious springs, warm summers, colorful falls, and winters with soft and short-lived snowfalls. Take our advice: Do *not* travel through here in the fall! The burning colors and brilliant oranges, yellows, and purples of the hardwood trees will break your heart with beauty.

What happened here to make quality retirement living such a bargain? First, an economic disaster occurred when the local coal mining industry automated and drastically eliminated jobs. Second, there was a public relations dilemma caused by the stereotypical view that coal mining country must be a landscape of dire poverty and trailer homes inhabited by uneducated and unfriendly natives. Trust me, none of the above apply to the Four Seasons Country!

It turns out that the highly unionized coal miners in this region were exceptionally well paid, had a high standard of living, and could afford any kind of homes they desired. Under those circumstances, who wants to live in a trailer? Therefore, substandard housing is rare in the Four Seasons Country area. As coal mining jobs were eliminated, workers received generous retirement benefits and severance pay. Many moved away after putting their homes on the market for whatever they could get. This depressed real estate prices to the point where high-quality homes on lovely landscaped lots became true bargains. We found exceptionally nice-looking communities with housing ranging from above average to exceptionally elegant. The countryside is dotted with small farms and sprawling Victorian homes as well as modern, California ranch–style homes. Choices range from gated golf-course developments to lovely, tree-shaded neighborhoods, all with a friendly, small-town ambiance. Above-average three-bedroom homes sell for about half the median price of homes in Florida, Arizona, or California, or even less. Larger, more upscale homes on landscaped and wooded parcels can be found for double that amount. We looked at a stately five-bedroom brick home on an acre of land that could have been purchased for $250,000.

The four towns specifically involved in the Four Seasons Country retirement recruitment project are the Virginia towns of Tazewell (pop. 4,200) and Richlands (pop. 6,000) and the West Virginia towns of Bluefield (pop. 14,000) and Princeton (pop. 7,000). Each of these communities has its own charms, and after interviewing residents and newcomers, we are convinced that relocation here could be a perfect solution for many retirees.

Appalachian Virginia and West Virginia Climate

	Jan.	Apr.	Jul.	Oct.	Average Annual Rain	Snow
Daily Highs	39°	65°	83°	65°	37"	48"
Daily Low	22°	47°	60°	39°		

For more information contact Richlands Chamber of Commerce, 1413 Front Street, Richlands, VA 24641; (540) 963–3385; www.2chambers.com/richlands,_virginia. htm; or Tazewell Chamber of Commerce, Tazewell Mall Box 6, Tazewell, VA 24651; (540) 988–5091; www.2chambers.com/ tazewell,_virginia.htm; or Greater Bluefield Chamber of Commerce, P.O. Box 4098, Bluefield, WV 24701; (304) 327–7184; Princeton Chamber of Commerce, 910 Oakvale Road, Princeton, WV 24740; (304) 487–1502.

BROOKINGS AND HARBOR, OREGON

These twin towns are typical of a string of retirement locations along Oregon's spectacular Pacific coast. As in all West Coast states, Oregon's beaches and oceanfront are public property, and although waterfront land may be privately owned (although much is state-owned), the public's access to the beachfront or water's edge cannot be restricted. These locations vary in size from villages to small cities. Some communities hold commercial possibilities for small business, and perhaps some limited employment opportunities. Like most smaller towns in Oregon, jobs can be found, but the wages will not be outstanding unless one has some extraordinary skills or talents. Volunteer jobs are available for retirees who can't stand being idle.

Brookings and Harbor sit on opposite banks of the Chetco River, not far north of the California state line. For all practical purposes these two small towns make one small city. Out of a population of 15,000, an estimated 30 percent are retirees.

All along the coast, mild weather is the theme—never freezing, never hot. Temperatures are always on the cool side, with sweaters just as comfortable in August as in January. Overcoats and heavy jackets seldom come out of the closet. Encouraged by mild, ice-free winters, flowers bloom all year along Oregon's coast. For years Brookings residents have boasted that their town is even warmer than their neighbor's, claiming the title of "banana belt" of the coast. Oddly enough, there's some truth to this. It seems to have something to do with high-pressure systems that tend to circle through this region with frequency. This occasionally makes temperatures here 4 or 5 degrees warmer than in nearby towns.

Like most towns on the Oregon coast, the populated areas of Brookings and Harbor occupy a relatively narrow strip along the coastline. Forested wilderness area and low mountains begin at the edge of town. In fact about 90 percent of the county is national forest, Bureau of Land Management, or lumber company property, and almost all of it is open to the public. This is good news for those who enjoy hiking, camping, hunting, and fishing.

Home prices vary along the Oregon coast, but not as much as in the interior. This is because all coastal communities partake of the same climate, ocean views, and cultural and recreational aspects. Although real estate in one area might be a bit higher than in another location, the differences aren't dramatic. In general housing on the Oregon coast is about 10 percent below national averages, but because there is so much ordinary construction and inexpensive housing, prices can be better than averages indicate.

Brookings and Harbor Climate

	Jan.	April	July	Oct.	Average Annual Rain	Snow
Daily Highs	55°	59°	68°	65°	73"	1"
Daily Lows	41°	43°	50°	48°		

For more information contact Brookings-Harbor Chamber of Commerce, P.O. Box 848, Brookings, OR 97415; (800) 535-9469; www.brookingsor.com.

BOONE AND BLOWING ROCK, NORTH CAROLINA

Nestled in a valley of the gorgeous Blue Ridge Mountains—some of the world's most scenic—the small city of Boone refers to itself as the "Heart of the High Country." And that it is. Boone is the region's most populous town, with about 13,500 inhabitants, plus a large student population (12,000) who attend Appalachian State University. Not all students live in town, of course; most of them commute daily from surrounding communities.

Boone's historic district, with century-old brick buildings, fits in perfectly with the Blue Ridge background. The surprisingly large downtown business district and a large strip-mall shopping center seem appropriate for a much larger city. This isn't surprising, since Boone is the major commercial center for the surrounding communities. We've enjoyed watching Boone grow from a small town into a small city over the years we've been visiting.

Nearby, you'll find numerous small towns and villages where you can blend into the daily routine and find yourself among friendly neighbors. The local folk, who proudly refer to themselves as "mountain people," are famous for their hospitality to "flatlanders." However, the number of outsiders moving in from various parts of the country is growing larger every day, and before long it's conceivable that flatlanders could outnumber the mountain people.

Picturesque Blowing Rock is the second-largest town in the area, with a population of 1,200. (That should tell you something about population density here.)

Actually, Blowing Rock could be better described as an exceptionally charming village rather than a town. Perched atop the Eastern Continental Divide, right on the Blue Ridge Parkway, Blowing Rock is known for its quaint shops, fabulous dining, and charming accommodations. In short, it's become a tourist-oriented artists' colony. Visitors come by the droves—so many that you'll have trouble finding a parking spot during the season. This extra traffic is the only downside we could find here.

The village name comes from a rock formation that juts precariously out and over a dramatic 3,000-foot drop to a valley below. A strong updraft of wind from the valley flows continually over the rock, hence the name "Blowing Rock." This is a picturesque and elegant place for all seasons: cool in the summer, dazzling in the fall, a Currier and Ives portrait in the winter, and a festival of wildflowers in the spring. The town features historic, heirloom homes in the style of the nineteenth century, exquisite yet rustic in design and construction. Many have been converted to bed-and-breakfasts and antiques shops.

Even though the region is somewhat isolated from Asheville (an hour's drive away), a surprising array of cultural activities is available to residents. Mayland College, located in nearby Spruce Pine, sponsors programs in many surrounding communities. Classes offered are pottery, studio glass, traditional weaving, jewelry making, iron working, and sculpture and bronze casting.

Boone and Blowing Rock Climate

	Jan.	April	July	Oct.	Average Annual Rain	Snow
Daily Highs	45°	68°	84°	68°	48"	17"
Daily Lows	26°	43°	62°	43°		

For more information contact Blowing Rock Chamber of Commerce, P.O. Box 406, Blowing Rock, NC 28605; (800) 295–7851

or (828) 295–7851; www.blowingrock.com; or Boone Convention & Visitors Bureau, 208 Howard Street, Boone, NC 28607-4037; (828) 262–3516 or (800) 852–9506; www.boonechamber.com.

DESERT HOT SPRINGS, CALIFORNIA

California's Palm Springs is a showcase of elegant desert living, with golf courses, gated communities, and movie stars living behind landscaped confines of their weekend homes. The dryness of the desert contrasts with the greenery of the residential areas. However, for most folks, the price of real estate makes living in Palm Springs all but impossible. If the posh atmosphere of Palm Springs is intimidating, you'll find a "Poor Man's Palm Springs" north across Interstate 10, about fifteen minutes away.

The affordable town of Desert Hot Springs (pop. 17,000) basks in the shadows of the Little San Bernardino Mountains in the background and shares many features of its high-priced neighbor. The town's name comes from the hot water that seeps beneath the ground from nearby mountain slopes. Homeowners commonly tap the steaming water and use it to fill their backyard swimming pools and hot tubs.

Because real estate is affordable here, residents enjoy affordable retirement living in a pleasant desert setting and have access to the fabled restaurants, golf courses, shopping, and social life of Palm Springs just a few minutes away. Because the elevation is 1,000 feet higher than Palm Springs, summer temperatures in Desert Hot Springs can be ten degrees lower than in communities on the valley floor. Winter days are often warmer because the nearby mountain peaks block the cold north winds that occasionally sweep down from Alaska. The most common weather complaint concerns annoying westerly winds that hit Desert Hot Springs but circumvent Palm Springs.

Unlike in Palm Springs, most people here are year-round residents rather than weekend visitors from nearby Los Angeles. Many are retired, but a large number are younger people who work in Palm Springs but can't afford to live there.

Desert Hot Springs Climate

	Jan.	April	July	Oct.	Average Annual Rain	Snow
Daily Highs	70°	87°	109°	92°	5"	0
Daily Lows	43°	54°	75°	60°		

For more information contact Desert Hot Springs Chamber of Commerce, 11-711 West Drive, Desert Hot Springs, CA 92240; (760) 329–6403; www.deserthotsprings. com.

DOTHAN, ALABAMA

The small city of Dothan (pop. 57,000) and its neighboring communities of Ozark and Enterprise combine to offer an interesting set of retirement choices for the unusually diverse retiree population that lives here. Folks relocate here from all over the world, so nonnatives don't feel out of place in this southeastern Alabama setting. This is partly due to nearby Fort Rucker, home of the world's largest international helicopter training center; military families from around the world remember Dothan when making retirement plans. Post-exchange privileges and access to military medical services make it a natural.

An interesting source of Dothan's unique diversity is a large colony of civilian retirees from the Panama Canal Zone. After the Canal was turned over to Panama, between 100 and 120 families relocated in Dothan to begin (or resume) the retirements they started in Panama. It all started some years ago, when a Canal Zone employee convinced his wife to retire in his home state of Alabama instead of staying in Panama, as most others were doing at that time. They moved here, liked what they saw, and began telling fellow employees. The Panama relocation movement grew from there.

Another source of out-of-state retirees is the region's retirement attraction committee, which works hard to get out the news of what the area has to offer: a high quality of life on an affordable budget. The committee showcases the area's well-kept neighborhoods, quiet, tree-shaded streets, and inexpensive homes on large lots. It also points out the low cost of living here, usually 10 percent below national averages; the cost of real estate is 25 percent below the national average at the time of writing. Alabama real estate taxes are among the lowest in the nation.

The town of Enterprise (pop. 21,000) is located near Fort Rucker and is military-oriented, and the town of Ozark (pop. 17,000), a dozen or so miles away, attracts retirees who love the stately homes on huge lots. One retiree from Ozark put it this way: "This area is the best of all worlds. We live far enough south to avoid winter cold and far enough away from the ocean to escape destructive humidity. We enjoy a small-town atmosphere, yet we're close to the Gulf Coast and great fishing."

Dothan Climate

	Jan.	April	July	Oct.	Average Annual Rain	Snow
Daily Highs	57°	77°	92°	78°	49"	0
Daily Lows	36°	53°	72°	53°		

For more information contact Dothan Area Chamber of Commerce, 440 Honeysuckle Road, Dothan, AL 36302; (334) 792–5138 or (800) 221–1027; www.enter prisealabama.com.

EUREKA AND ARCATA, CALIFORNIA

If you are looking for an area where it never freezes or snows and where you never have heat waves, this is the region for your relocation. Of all the places we've researched, this part of California has the most even, year-round temperature range. The weather is continually cool, where one has to wear a sweater every day of the year. Check out the temperature chart below. You'll see that there's only a seven-degree difference in afternoon temperatures in January and July!

The northern California city of Eureka is bordered on one side by beautiful Humboldt Bay and on the other by mountains lush with redwood forests, a reminder of the area's rich logging heritage. Eureka owes its boomtown start to the gold rush back in 1850, when its location on Humboldt Bay made it ideal as a port to supply mines in the mountains to the east, in Trinity County. Eureka flourished overnight as gold seekers poured into the port fresh from San Francisco. Arcata, on the northern edge of the bay, was founded about the same time. Once the gold rush was over, Eureka settled back into a time warp, with a character that peaked out in Victorian times. Because many early settlers were lumber barons, you can imagine the care and attention to detail with which the artisans constructed their ornate homes. As a result, Eureka's Victorian architecture rivals some of San Francisco's best historic neighborhoods. The entire town has been declared a state historical landmark.

Lumber and fishing in Humboldt Bay are the mainstays of Eureka's economy nowadays. More than 300 fishing vessels call this port home, hauling in more rockfish, crab, oysters, and shrimp than in any other fishing port in California. We love strolling along Eureka's quaint Old Town waterfront, breathing in the fresh sea air, and watching boats returning with catches of salmon and tasty Dungeness crab.

Although its population is only 28,000, Eureka is the center, culturally and commercially, of another 50,000 residents in the immediate area. In fact, 86 percent of Humboldt County's 130,000 people live within a 20-mile radius of Eureka. The famous Redwood Empire forests begin near the edge of town and climb the mountains beyond, a wilderness area with great trout streams and wildlife such as deer, river otters, and herons.

To give you an idea of the affordable cost of real estate here, the average price of a house in Eureka is $121,000 at the time of writing. In a similar San Francisco neighborhood, that might buy a garage. To buy a livable home in San Francisco, you'd have to multiply that amount by five.

Arcata is a combination retirement town and university town. Today's population is 18,000, plus 7,500 students at Humboldt State University, one of the area's economic mainstays. The school is the source of many cultural and entertainment productions open to the public. The academic atmosphere complements an old-fashioned, Victorian atmosphere of Arcata, a place where mountains, forest, and blue Pacific all come together.

Mobile homes are located away from the city's residential sections and seem to be in abundant supply because they sell at very reasonable prices. In the countryside, many mobile homes are placed on spacious wooded lots.

Eureka and Arcata Climate

	Jan.	April	July	Oct.	Average Annual Rain	Snow
Daily Highs	53°	55°	60°	60°	39"	0
Daily Lows	41°	44°	52°	48°		

For more information contact Arcata Eureka Chamber of Commerce, 1635 Heindon Road, Arcata, CA 95521; (707) 822-3619; www.arcatachamber.com.

FAIRHOPE, ALABAMA

Often referred to as "Mobile's bedroom community," the town of Fairhope (pop. 13,000) is only a 15-mile commute from the thriving city of Mobile. Employees of corporations and industry in Mobile love to escape to Fairhope, with its moss-draped live oaks and panoramic views of Mobile Bay. Fairhope's charming and lively downtown is often compared with California's Carmel-by-the Sea, the way it entices visitors and tourists for antiques shopping, strolling, and dining. Oysters, shrimp, and crab from the nearby Gulf of Mexico are favorite delicacies served by small cafes and restaurants in the area. Nearby communities of Montrose, Point Clear, and Daphne also serve as homes for commuters and out-of-state retirees.

The beachside communities of Gulf Shores and Orange Beach are not far from Fairhope, yet they offer completely different lifestyles on Alabama's only stretch of Gulf beachfront, fast becoming a choice destination for golf enthusiasts and saltwater anglers. The 32-mile beach is Alabama's only window to the Gulf of Mexico, and it clearly matches anything Florida has to offer. Local people like to call it "Alabama's Gulf Coast Riviera."

Thousands of winter escapees from the north flock here for the season, and summer tourism is growing, a boost to the local economy. Gulf Shores (pop. 5,000) and Orange Beach (pop. 3,000) are seeing some developments, including luxury golf housing, make an appearance to accommodate newcomers. Commuting from the beaches to a job in Mobile is not out of the question.

Fairhope Climate

	Jan.	April	July	Oct.	Average Annual Rain	Snow
Daily Highs	61°	77°	90°	79°	61"	0
Daily Lows	49°	60°	74°	66°		

For more information contact Fairhope Chamber of Commerce, 327 Fairhope Avenue, Fairhope, AL 36532; (251) 928-6387; www.eschamber.com; or Orange Beach Welcome Center, 23685 Perdido Beach Boulevard, Orange Beach, AL 36561; (251) 974-1510 or (800) 982-8562; www.yourtownchamber.com/chamber/al chamber/orangebeachchamber.html.

FLORIDA KEYS

The Florida Keys, a jumbled string of tropical islands and reefs hanging from the tip of Florida, is the southernmost part of the continental United States. It is also the ultimate getaway for those who seek an easy escape from the mundane world of work and conventional living. The Keys are a merger of warm blue waters, exotic foliage, great restaurants, and parties that never cease, with the town of Key West as the pearl in the oyster. President Harry Truman loved Key West so much that he maintained his winter White House here. After a particularly difficult day, he once said, "I've a notion to move the White House to Key West and just stay!" Certain types of retirees, those who are adventurous and young at heart, thoroughly enjoy the Caribbean feel of this island paradise, so different that it's easy to imagine you are in a different country. Long-time residents refer to their island region as "the Conch Republic," and to themselves as "Conchs." They issue conch passports and maintain a Web site for the republic (www.conch republic.com).

Key West (pop. 26,000) is the largest of the towns sprinkled along the archipelago. The highway leading south from the mainland follows the route of an old railway line, an engineering marvel in itself, 110 miles to the last of the accessible islands and the city of Key West. The highway skips from one coral atoll to another over numerous causeways and bridges, crossing islands festooned with palm trees, hibiscus, and bougainvillea and bearing such romantic names as Key Largo, Islamorada, and Matacumbre. Boating and fishing are top attractions, along with snorkeling and diving. Here you'll find one of the longest living reefs in the Western Hemisphere, with crystal-clear waters and visibility up to 100 feet, with more than 500 wrecks to explore.

Yachts are "in" throughout the Keys, large ones and small ones. Resident sailors simply cut berths into the coral and limestone backyards of their homes and tie up. Other houses are set back against networks of canals, where their occupants can dock after a day's adventure of fishing or treasure hunting in the warm waters of the Gulf Stream. On both Key Largo and Marathon, we checked out several homes, some with canals at their backs, where motorboats, launches, and yachts were tied to individual docks. We even found mobile homes with sloops moored to floating patios.

Local residents bemoan the fact that so many tourists and college students overrun Key West, making everywhere so crowded that locating a parking place becomes a treasure hunt. Key West's tolerant acceptance of alternate lifestyles and the residents' "live and let live" attitude has seen the establishment of a sizable gay community that coexists amiably with Key West's laid-back citizenry.

Popularity has taken its toll, and demand has boosted prices, yet compared with the really expensive parts of the country, Key West homes look affordable. Most of the other towns in the Keys have much lower prices, often under national averages, which is understandable, since construction is less expensive.

Florida Keys Climate

	Jan.	April	July	Oct.	Average Annual Rain	Snow
Daily Highs	72°	82°	89°	84°	39"	0
Daily Lows	66°	73°	80°	76°		

For more information contact Key West Chamber of Commerce, 402 Wall Street, Key West, FL 33040; (305) 294–2587; www.keywestchamber.org.

GREEN VALLEY, ARIZONA

The adult community of Green Valley, about 25 miles south of Tucson, started off as an unlikely development on an elevated piece of desert land, miles from anywhere (the Interstate hadn't been constructed at that point) and not a shopping center in sight. The one thing the land had going for it was lovely desert scenery and a higher elevation than Tucson, giving Green Valley cooler summers. The development sits at an altitude of 2,900 feet at the foot of the Santa Rita Mountains (an Apache hangout in the old days). Residents boast that summer temperatures are consistently five degrees cooler than Tucson and ten degrees cooler than Phoenix. Because of the low humidity, during the warmest part of summer, night temperatures cool down almost thirty degrees below the afternoon's high, making it possible to sleep without the air conditioner running.

The Green Valley concept turned out to be not so unlikely after all. Today more than 24,000 people call Green Valley home, the overwhelming majority retirees. Four shopping centers and more than 350 businesses serve Green Valley residents, including several supermarkets, two major drugstores, discount department stores, apparel stores, restaurants, and many specialty shops. Tucson International Airport is only 23 miles away.

The community is unincorporated, and folks seem to prefer it that way: lower taxes, fewer bureaucrats, and more time for golf. A study of the local telephone directory clearly demonstrates the melting-pot character of Green Valley. In addition to phone numbers and addresses, the local directory lists the residents' former hometowns as well as their occupations before retirement. The directory lists retirees from all fifty of the United States and ten Canadian provinces, as well as residents from several foreign countries, including Costa Rica, England, France, Ireland, Germany, and Sweden.

Green Valley Climate

	Jan.	April	July	Oct.	Average Annual Rain	Snow
Daily Highs	65°	82°	98°	82°	12"	2"
Daily Lows	39°	50°	70°	56°		

For more information contact Green Valley Chamber of Commerce, 270 West Continental Road, Suite 100, Green Valley, AZ 85614; (520) 625–7575; www.green valleyazchamber.com.

KERRVILLE, TEXAS

Northwest of San Antonio and west of Austin, the Texas landscape turns into rolling hills, mostly wooded and intersected by a half dozen swift-flowing rivers, spring-fed creeks, and lakes. This has become a popular place for retirement, with the town of Kerrville claiming to be the capital of the region known as Texas Hill Country. With about one-third of its residents qualifying as senior citizens, Kerrville has all the desirable features of a retirement town, including a veterans' hospital, a liberal arts college, master-planned country clubs,

quality mobile-home communities, miles of hiking and biking trails, and a low cost of living.

One thing that makes the region different from other parts of West Texas is a dependable year-round rainfall. The Hill Country receives more than 30 inches of rain each year. That isn't an extraordinary amount, yet it's several times that of many Southwest locations. This accounts for its green, sometimes lush vegetation. The rain falls every month of the year, helping to keep things looking fresh. Kerrville's location at 1,600 to 1,800 feet above sea level moderates the climate, providing cooler summers and more clearly defined seasons than either Austin or San Antonio.

With a population of almost 20,000, Kerrville is the Hill Country's major shopping destination. Being close to Interstate 10, some residents find it convenient to commute to jobs in San Antonio, about 45 minutes away. Thus, Kerrville fulfills two roles: as a place to retire and as a bedroom community for Austin and San Antonio.

Another popular retirement possibility in the Hill Country not far down the highway is the village of Wimberley (pop. 2,500). The community consistently receives excellent reviews in retirement magazines as a prime retirement destination. The town's photogenic qualities make wonderful color layouts for these magazines. This is where the clear, cool waters of Cypress Creek join the warmer waters of the slow-moving Blanco River, a place where large trees and old homes of native stone hark back to another era. Wimberley sits at an altitude of 1,100 feet—twice as high as Austin—and enjoys slightly cooler summers and a few more inches of rainfall. As in other towns in this part of the country, snow is a rarity. Commuting to Austin and San Antonio is relatively easy.

Kerrville Climate

	Jan.	April	July	Oct.	Average Annual Rain	Snow
Daily Highs	56°	77°	90°	79°	30"	2"
Daily Lows	36°	57°	74°	59°		

For more information contact Kerrville Area Chamber of Commerce, 1700 Sidney Baker Street, Suite 100, Kerrville, TX 78028; (830) 896-1155; www.kerrvilletx.com; or Wimberley Chamber of Commerce, P.O. Box 12, Wimberley, TX 78676; (512) 847-2201; www.texasoutside.com/wimberleychamberofcommerce.htm.

MOUNTAIN HOME, ARKANSAS

A popular relocation destination for retirees from the Midwest sits in the north-central region of Arkansas, along the Missouri border. This is a picturesque area of forests, lakes, and rivers in the geographical center of the Ozark Mountains, 15 miles south of the Missouri state line. A cluster of peaceful towns has become a miniature population melting pot; retirees relocate here from all over the country. Even traditional retirement hot spots such as California and Florida send their citizens here to retire. Besides a scenic wonderland of lakes and low mountains, residents brag about an exceptionally low crime rate, inexpensive living, and friendly neighbors with common interests and backgrounds. One retired couple from Indiana said, "We wanted a small town, not too congested, with a good hospital and reasonable living costs. Real estate prices here are all over the place. Wealthy people who can afford the best lake frontage properties can easily spend up to a million for homes, but we common folk have no trouble finding a decent place for around $30,000 to $75,000."

Three places here draw the retirees: the towns of Mountain Home and Bull Shoals and the village of Lakeview. They are arranged near the shores of Bull Shoals Lake, which stretches for more than 1,000 miles. The wooded surroundings and deep, blue waters are legendary among bass fishermen. The rivers and creeks feeding the lake are considered prime locations for rainbow trout. There are no closed seasons here; you can fish year-round. The lake's shore is off-limits to construction up to the highwater mark, yet the public has free access. This keeps the shoreline from being cluttered with scruffy-looking boathouses and sagging docks and preserves the lake's pristine, natural look.

Mountain Home is the largest town, with a population of about 10,000, and serves as the region's major shopping center. It's the only community with a real downtown, including an old-fashioned town square. Mountain Home happens to be in one of the few counties in northern Arkansas that isn't "dry"; it is renowned for restaurants that serve cocktails and wine with dinner.

Mountain Home Climate

	Jan.	April	July	Oct.	Average Annual Rain	Snow
Daily Highs	48°	74°	94°	76°	40"	7"
Daily Lows	27°	49°	71°	49°		

For more information contact Mountain Home Area Chamber of Commerce, Highway 412/62 East, Mountain Home, AR 72654-0488; (800) 822-3536 or (870) 425-5111; www.enjoymountainhome.com.

NATCHITOCHES, LOUISIANA

A few years ago we happened to discover the charming little city of Natchitoches (pronounced NAK-a-tish) while researching towns with the help of Louisiana's retirement welcoming program. The director of the state program invited us to visit Natchitoches, and we immediately fell in love with the place.

History buffs will find this fascinating little city of 18,000 absolutely stunning. It has one of the most picturesque and authentic historic downtown sections of any place we've yet seen, reminiscent of the French Quarter in New Orleans, yet more authentic. In fact the entire town is a historic treasure, with homes dating from before the American Revolution rather commonplace. To get a flavor of what Natchitoches looks and feels like, rent the movie *Steel Magnolias* from your local video store. The motion picture was filmed on location in the town, using homes in the downtown area as stage sets. Local residents were hired as extras.

Here's an astounding fact: Natchitoches is the *oldest* settlement in the entire Louisiana Territory, predating even New Orleans! French explorers and traders made contact with the Natchitoches Indians in the year 1700, and fourteen years later established a trading outpost on the Red River. Natchitoches soon became a bustling river port and an important crossroads of trade. Wealthy planters not only built imposing plantation houses along the river but also maintained elegant showplaces in town. Many of these homes are private residences today. We were so impressed that we seriously considered buying a second home there ourselves.

Natchitoches's potential as a good retirement choice is enhanced by the presence of Northwestern State University of Louisiana. In addition to its symphony, dinner theater, ballet performances, and other entertainment, the school offers interesting continuing education programs for mature adults. Real estate costs in Louisiana are among the lowest in the nation; prices in Natchitoches, while being several notches above ordinary Louisiana towns, are low enough to get you a fabulous, historic home for the price of a tract home in many other states.

Natchitoches Climate

	Jan.	April	July	Oct.	Average Annual Rain	Snow
Daily Highs	57°	79°	94°	80°	56"	0
Daily Lows	35°	58°	72°	56°		

For more information contact Natchitoches Area Chamber of Commerce, PO Box 3, Natchitoches, LA 71458; (318) 352-6894; www.natchitocheschamber.com.

PINEHURST AND SOUTHERN PINES, NORTH CAROLINA

Golfers considering an in-depth golf retirement can't do much better than the North Carolina villages of Pinehurst and Southern Pines. These delightful small towns (some 25,000 inhabitants, including the nearby town of Aberdeen) offer a choice of forty golf courses within a 16-mile radius, some among the most highly rated in the country. One of the original golf courses, designed in 1907, is routinely ranked among the top ten golf courses in the world.

Located halfway between New York and Florida and midway between the Appalachian Mountains and the Atlantic Ocean, in the region known as the Sandhills area, Pinehurst and Southern Pines are within a few hours' drive of the metropolitan cities of Raleigh (the state capital) and Charlotte. Before the towns became popular retirement destinations, most travelers thought of the villages simply as convenient stopover places on their way to their Florida vacations. Here was the logical place to break up the trip at the halfway mark and stay over a day or two for a few rounds of golf. As retirement time drew nearer, some naturally began thinking more about Southern Pines and Pinehurst and less about Florida.

These villages are clearly of upscale residential quality, with some truly magnificent homes, yet they are not gated as are many country club–type developments.

The neighborhoods are open; anyone can cruise through the streets without having to be a resident. This is not a problem, because crime levels in the Pinehurst–Southern Pines region are very low. Newcomers who buy existing homes in some neighborhoods automatically secure a membership in one of the country clubs as part of the purchase price of their property. (They secure the monthly fees as well.) This is an important feature because some golf-club developments have long waiting lists for membership.

Because the elevation here is higher than the eastern portions of the Carolinas, summers aren't quite as warm or humid. But even the cool January days permit year-round outdoor activities. "Any day it's not raining, I can golf, hike, or ride horseback," said a retiree here. "When I lived in Florida, it was too damned muggy in the summer!"

Pinehurst and Southern Pines Climate

	Jan.	April	July	Oct.	Average Annual Rain	Snow
Daily Highs	55°	74°	91°	75°	50"	4"
Daily Lows	34°	47°	68°	50°		

For more information contact Pinehurst Visitors Bureau, 395 Magnolia Road, Pinehurst, NC 28374; (910) 692-3330 or (800) 346-5362; www.homeofgolf.com; or Sandhills Area Chamber of Commerce, 10677 Highway 15-501 North, Pinehurst, NC 28388; (910) 692-3926; www.sandhills chamber.com; or Village of Pinehurst Chamber of Commerce, 395 Magnolia Road, Pinehurst, NC 28374; (910) 295-1900; www.villageofpinehurst.org.

PORT CHARLOTTE, FLORIDA

A few miles north of Fort Myers on the shore of Charlotte Harbor, the cities of Punta Gorda and Port Charlotte offer a

Real estate prices may determine where you move, but don't let inexpensive housing costs be the major factor in your decision. All too often, the reason for low home prices is that nobody in their right mind wants to move there! When everybody wants to sell and nobody wants to buy, there could be a good reason. Find out why!

unique retirement lifestyle. Beaches aren't the big deal here; residents focus instead on the miles of canals that cut through their neighborhoods like boulevards. More than 150 miles of man-made waterways provide access to the Gulf of Mexico for boating and fishing enthusiasts. As one resident pointed out, "The water is so clean and unpolluted here, we don't hesitate to swim or water-ski in our own backyards."

Having a boat tied up in the backyard is as common as having an automobile in the garage. You'll notice some rather ordinary houses backed up to the waterways with more money invested in the motorboat than the total value of the home. Boaters are quick to point out, however, that waterways in neighborhoods on the west of the Tamiami Trail—the main highway that bisects Port Charlotte—must pass under low bridges. So only boats with low profiles—motorboats or small sailboats with masts that can be dismantled—can make their way to salt water. If you're a fan of tall-masted ships, better look on the saltwater side of the river—otherwise you'll never make it out to open water.

Port Charlotte is large (pop. about 95,000) but it doesn't give you a city feeling. The town spreads out along the Tamiami Trail (U.S. Highway 41), with businesses and malls scattered along the highway rather than concentrated in a downtown civic center. Just a block or so off the main thoroughfare, tranquil neighborhoods offer peaceful havens. From here south along the 30 miles of highway to Fort Myers, you'll find several impressive mobile-home developments. Some are country clubs in every sense of the term, and the prices are equal to what you might pay for a conventional house, yet in a country club setting. In these developments you purchase the lot that your mobile home sits on.

Port Charlotte Climate

	Jan.	April	July	Oct.	Average Annual Rain	Snow
Daily Highs	74°	85°	91°	85°	54"	0
Daily Lows	53°	62°	74°	68°		

For more information contact Charlotte County Chamber of Commerce, 326 West Marion Avenue, Suite 112, Punta Gorda, FL 33950; (941) 639-2222; www.charlotte countychamber.org.

RUIDOSO, NEW MEXICO

When travelers enter the small mountain city of Ruidoso for the first time, they are in for a surprise. Ruidoso is not a setting one expects to encounter in New Mexico. As the mountain highway winds upward, the landscape changes almost magically from dry desert covered with brush and dusty patches of *carrizo* grass into a picturesque river canyon shaded by majestic evergreens perfuming the air. Cool mountain breezes and lush vegetation make Californians think of Lake Tahoe. Easterners might recall Maine forests or Canadian mountain vistas.

Of course this isn't news to west Texans; they've known about the Ruidoso Upper Canyon for decades as an excellent place to escape blazing Texas summers and as an eventual retirement location. The crystal-clear river cascading through the tree-

"Northern" vs. "Southern" Climates

Hotter summers in the South? Look at the chart and compare a few northern cities with some located in the South. Note the number of days below freezing and the number of days over 90 degrees. In some cases there are fewer over-90 days in southern cities, but the significant difference is the number of days below freezing in the North. Southern summers last longer, which makes them only *seem* hotter.

Southern Cities	Average Humidity	Days Over 90°F	Days Under 32°F	July Avg. High	July Avg. Low
Atlanta, Georgia	70%	19	59	86°	69°
Birmingham, Alabama	72%	39	60	88°	70°
Clarksville, Tennessee	71%	37	75	90°	69°
Memphis, Tennessee	69%	64	59	88°	72°
Northern Cities					
Kansas City, Missouri	69%	40	106	83°	69°
Wichita, Kansas	66%	62	114	87°	70°

shaded canyon gives the town its name, because *ruidoso* is Spanish for "noisy," a good description of the sound of river water cascading over rocks in the canyon.

Summer cabins nestled among the large ponderosa pines have a way of being enlarged for full-time retirement living, and newer homes start springing up for both retirees and working families. This continuing growth provides employment for even more new residents and encourages more businesses to open. Ruidoso has blossomed into a pleasant town of about 7,500 inhabitants and is still growing, with the county population pushing 13,000. The area supports many more shops, restaurants, and businesses of all kinds than you might expect of a town this size.

With the opening of the racetrack at Ruidoso Downs in 1947, people started thinking of Ruidoso as a resort instead of merely a summertime mountain getaway. Then with the development of a ski run high up on Apache Peak, Ruidoso's reputation as a winter resort was established, making the community a year-round resort and a great place for retirement. This is the southernmost area to ski in the Southwest, and because of its exceptionally high location, skiing lasts long after many other areas have closed down, providing some of the best warm-weather powder skiing in the world.

A tall evergreen forest creates a properly rustic setting for Ruidoso real estate, with homes shaded by a thick green canopy. Most are casually located in a somewhat hodgepodge way. Elegant homes can sit next door to small cottages, log cabins, and, sometimes, mobile homes on private lots. The higher end of the housing scale, at the northern edge of town, is also at the highest elevation.

Ruidoso Climate

	Jan.	April	July	Oct.	Average Annual Rain	Snow
Daily Highs	50°	65°	81°	67°	21"	44"
Daily Lows	17°	28°	48°	31°		

For more information contact Ruidoso Valley Chamber of Commerce, 20 Sudderth Drive, Ruidoso, NM 88355; (877) 784–3676; www.ruidoso.net.

SUN CITY HILTON HEAD, SOUTH CAROLINA

Retirement on the fabulous island of Hilton Head is something more or less reserved for the affluent, and it becomes more expensive as time goes by. But take heart: You probably *can* afford the Del Webb Corporation's Sun City Hilton Head retirement development, even though Sun City Hilton Head isn't actually *on* Hilton Head Island, just nearby. The development is located some 13 miles from the ocean in Bluffton, yet it's a great place for retirement, and the Hilton Head designation adds a certain amount of class to your new hometown address.

So far Sun City has built 1,600 homes in what was once a South Carolina pine forest, and it is adding homes at the rate of 500 each year. When the 5,600-acre project is completed, Sun City will have 16,000 year-round residents. Don't worry, it won't be exactly urban, because 35 percent of the development is dedicated to lakes, wooded areas, and green belts. Like other Del Webb projects, this one features golf and tennis and emphasizes an active lifestyle.

This new development fulfills much of the original Del Webb Arizona concept, but with a motif adapted to South Carolina's gracious southern traditions. The community is focused on a town center designed to resemble a traditional southern town square, complete with a picturesque clock tower. The village center offers indoor/outdoor swimming pools, a tennis club, bocce courts, a bowling center, a huge fitness complex, and other amenities you would expect to find in a Sun City community.

The advantage to this type of retirement—besides quality surroundings and excellent facilities—is the carefully planned social structure already in place when newcomers move in. You'll find instant involvement in bridge clubs, golf foursomes, hobbies, travel clubs, and much more. It eases the effort of making new friends in an adopted community. Everything is in place for you to start a new life.

Sun City Hilton Head Climate

	Jan.	April	July	Oct.	Average Annual Rain	Snow
Daily Highs	59°	76°	89°	77°	49"	0
Daily Lows	41°	58°	75°	60°		

For more information contact Sun City Hilton Head, 127 Sun City Lane, Bluffton, SC 29910; (800) 978-9781; www.delwebb.com/activeadult/southcarolina/suncityhiltonhead.

COLLEGE TOWN RELOCATION

After several years of researching communities for our retirement guidebooks, we began to notice something rather curious. It appeared that most of our favorite places happened to feature a college or university. At first we assumed that this was a coincidence. Basically, we liked each of these towns for their personalities and individual traits, things that didn't appear to have anything to do with the presence of a school.

When analyzing why we liked some towns better than others, we found that the places we preferred usually had a lively, user-friendly downtown center. Places we liked best often had a town square or central park, maybe with large trees and quality shopping, good restaurants, and sometimes a bookstore that offers entertainment or readings by authors. The town square usually has park benches, a movie theater, boutiques, and perhaps a restaurant or two with tables on the sidewalk where you can have a coffee and watch the world go by. But these things have nothing to do with a town having a college or university. Or do they?

Before long, we put it together: Even though an attractive town center makes a town more livable, it's the presence of the *college* that makes the town center different! College towns seem to be suspended in the past, in a sort of time warp. You feel like you've stepped back in time, entering an old-fashioned small town of forty years

ago. Back then, "downtown" was the central focus of the community. That's where residents would go shopping, meet friends for lunch, browse the bookstore, or maybe take in a movie matinee. The center of town was alive. Something was always happening.

What caused the demise of small-town America? About forty years ago, towns and small cities all over the nation began undergoing profound change. National chain stores and businesses found it very cost-effective to buy cheaper land on the edge of towns and build huge shopping centers. They covered fields with asphalt parking lots and constructed large buildings. Merchants in the downtown area could not compete with the low prices and convenience of the shopping malls, so they either joined the movement to the mall or closed their doors.

Many smaller cities were left with forlorn business centers, abandoned buildings, empty storefronts, and maybe only a few second-hand stores as relics of a once-thriving town center. To be sure, some communities have made heroic efforts to reverse the trend, but businesses that do relocate in the town center are different types, and most downtown areas will never return to their position as the social and commercial center of the community.

Why haven't college towns suffered this fate? The answer lies in the demographics. It turns out that students and faculty are not overly fond of hanging out at malls. That's not their nature. They prefer a lively, user-friendly downtown, within walking distance of the campus. Of course, to go to a supermarket or to buy a refrigerator, they may have to visit the mall. But when they want to buy a sweater, have lunch with friends, or listen to a jazz combo in a pub, they think "downtown."

In many college towns the population of students, faculty, and staff exceeds the number of noncollege residents. With several thousand students, faculty, and school employees as downtown customers, this means plenty of business for the town center. As long as the town center has customers, there will be stores and businesses.

The reverse of this axiom is also valid: As long as there are stores and businesses, other residents will join the university crowd in shopping, socializing, and dining. You might even find the old-fashioned single-screen movie theater—maybe showing foreign or classic films rather than first-run movies. College towns have an additional advantage: FBI crime statistics show that crime rates are much lower than in similar-sized towns where a college or university has no influence.

College towns are not just for retirement—they also are great places for working couples and families for several reasons, not the least of which is that these communities' towns are recession-resistant. In an ordinary town, when the national economy slides into the pits, businesses, factories, and retailers reduce costs by eliminating jobs. Unemployed people naturally cut back on spending, which hurts stores, restaurants, and businesses of all sorts, causing them to cut back even more. This results in even more unemployment. This chain reaction doesn't usually happen in college towns because the major

employer is the college or university. The number of students remains the same. The number of professors remains the same, as well as the number of office and maintenance staff. For these reasons, most university jobs are secure, and salaries remain constant despite outside economic conditions. Faculty, staff, and students see no reason to stop buying or spending simply because other communities are struggling through a weak economy. Yes, it's true that during the summer break many students return home, and businesses that cater to students have a slack period. This doesn't affect the economy because the employees who lose their temporary jobs are usually students who will be going home for the summer anyway.

Following are some college towns we like, places influenced by the presence of the school and its students, faculty, and staff. These aren't the only nice college towns around—you'll find others scattered throughout the nation. These are the places we've researched and feel like we can recommend for relocation. Doing your own investigation could easily turn up a setting that better suits your taste in climate, recreation, and special features.

ASHLAND, OREGON

One of our personal favorites is Ashland, Oregon, set in southern Oregon's gently rolling hills, with the snow-covered mountains of the Cascade Range looming in the distance. Cattle ranches and dairy farms begin at the edges of town, interspersed with remnants of the thick pine forests that once covered the region.

Ashland is an excellent relocation choice for outdoors-oriented people. Great hunting, fishing, and skiing are readily available, and crystal-clear rivers teeming with salmon and steelhead trout flow nearby. We're convinced that this region enjoys one of the best climates in the nation, with pleasant summers, mild winters, and only a third to a half the rainfall (20 inches annually) found in most of the eastern part of the continent. It's wonderfully sunny here most of the year.

Ashland's population of 20,000 is just the right size, with a balance between the university's 4,800 students plus another 4,000 local and regional students in the school's extended education program. The school is located near Ashland's charming downtown section and supports several excellent restaurants—ranging from Thai food to French country cooking to traditional pizza parlors—as well as bookstores, boutiques, and everything necessary to make a town center appealing. For major shopping, the city of Medford (pop. 65,000) is only fifteen minutes away via Interstate 5.

Like most college towns, Ashland enjoys an exceptionally low crime rate, according to FBI statistics. Residential neighborhoods here display a lovely blend of Victorian and modern, creating an unmistakable ambience of a university town. Ashland is famous for its unusual cultural amenities, particularly those sponsored by the school's drama department. Thousands of theater lovers from all over the country attend the renowned Ashland Shakespeare Festival. Local residents are given the opportunity to participate in the production, sometimes with minor stage roles.

As a final incentive, real estate costs are typical of Oregon, ranging from cheap to affordable, although—as with Oregon real estate in general—prices have risen somewhat in the last few years.

Ashland Climate

	Jan.	April	July	Oct.	Average Annual Rain	Snow
Daily Highs	45°	64°	91°	69°	20"	8"
Daily Lows	30°	37°	54°	40°		

For more information contact Ashland Chamber of Commerce, 110 East Main Street, Ashland, OR 97520; (541) 482–3486; www.ashlandchamber.com.

CLOSE-UP
School Involvement in the Community

Most universities take pride in providing the community with a wealth of entertainment and activities, much of it free or at affordable prices. These include football and basketball games and other sporting events. Plays and musicals typically are produced by the drama department, using not just drama students but often starring actors from the community, sometimes with a lot of professional experience. Regular lecture series present national and international personalities, the movers and shakers of politics and science. Concerts and musical recitals usually are presented by the music department. Many other cultural programs are given for the benefit of local residents. Few big cities provide the cultural entertainment that can match a small-town university's programs. Actually, the school depends on the community to provide audiences for many of these events, because students often prefer to spend Saturday nights dancing to a band at the local pizza joint rather than attending a Bach string quartet recital.

ATHENS, GEORGIA

About 70 miles east-northeast of Atlanta, not far from the foothills of the Blue Ridge Mountains, this university city of 106,000 residents combines a unique blend of Southern heritage and contemporary entertainment. The city is famous for its historic districts, featuring antebellum, Victorian, and other period homes.

Athens is a prime example of how a university can shape a community's architecture, business structure, and social ambiance. The restored downtown area looks exactly as a university town should look. The main street is arched over by large trees and lined with old-fashioned cast-iron lampposts with glass globes. Sidewalk tables and chairs in front of cafes invite residents to linger over a cup of coffee. Students, residents, and tourists stroll the streets, browse stores and shop, or simply sit on wrought-iron benches, observing the passing world with an unhurried casualness found only in a laid-back college town.

The region enjoys a moderate four-season climate with cool winters, colorful falls, and long, warm, and humid summers. Athens's population is large for a college town, yet the University of Georgia's 26,000 students clearly exert a beneficial influence on the community. Residents as well as visitors from nearby communities come to browse bookstores and specialty shops for articles not normally found in small Georgia cities. Visitors love to dine in the restaurants of downtown Athens, which specialize not only in traditional Southern-style cooking but also wood-fired pizza, Mexican enchiladas, Indian tandoori, Japanese cuisine, and, of course, the traditional student staple, hamburgers.

Several delightful neighborhoods are sprinkled with Greek Revival mansions and Victorians, interspersed with modern ranch-style homes and bungalows. An occasional antebellum homestead with massive columns and magnolia-shaded gardens reminds us of the lifestyle of the planter class of the Old South.

Because of the large student population, visiting scholars, and temporary faculty, Athens has an above-average number of apartments, condos, and rental homes available. The University of Georgia can be relied upon as a source of year-round athletic events, everything from football and basketball to intramural sports. Tuition is free for Georgia students and senior citizens. As one might expect, the cost of living is well below national averages, with housing well below average costs.

Athens Climate

	Jan.	April	July	Oct.	Average Annual Rain	Snow
Daily Highs	62°	75°	91°	74°	48"	2"
Daily Lows	33°	51°	70°	51°		

For more information contact Convention & Visitors Bureau, 280 East Dougherty Street, Athens, GA 30601; (706) 353-1820; www.visitathensga.com.

BOULDER, COLORADO

We can heartily recommend Boulder as one of our favorite university towns. The immediate surroundings are as beautiful as one could imagine: snow-covered peaks looming in the background and Rocky Mountain National Park just minutes away. Skiing and other winter sports are superb, summers are typically Colorado-perfect. For big-city convenience, Denver is only 27 miles away.

The University of Colorado, of course, is the centerpiece of this small city of 95,000. The university, students, and faculty affect the city's environment in several pleasant ways, infusing the institution's intellectual excitement into the community as a whole.

You don't have to be a registered student to attend lectures and speeches (often free) given by famous scientists, politicians, and other well-known personalities. Concerts ranging from Beethoven to bluegrass are presented by guest artists as well as the university's music department. Anyone can attend the school's stage plays, musicals, and Shakespeare productions with season tickets that cost less than a single performance at a New York theater.

The university's influence is most obvious in downtown Boulder, especially as you stroll along Pearl Street, the city's renovated downtown pedestrian mall. Mimes, jugglers, and musicians entertain, creating a magical scene that you'd expect to find in San Francisco or Paris rather than Colorado. This is the place to meet for coffee, read a newspaper or magazine, or perhaps browse a bookstore or a boutique. Pearl Street offers a great selection of good restaurants, art galleries, and specialty shops, of a variety and quality seldom seen in downtown areas of most other cities.

Statistically, Boulder's winters look bad—if you consider snow bad—because Boulder receives even more snow than Denver. December and February catch the heaviest blankets of the white stuff, but like Denver, daily temperatures climb high enough to get rid of it quickly. Even in winter, most days are warm enough to enjoy walking, biking, or other outdoor activities. Ski enthusiasts will be happy to learn there's a choice of ten ski areas within 110 miles of town. Summer provides gloriously sunny and comfortable days. The cost of living is above average, with housing costs particularly high, but the ambience is well worth paying a little more for a home.

Among the outstanding cultural events offered by the university is its Shakespeare festival, one of the top three in the country. There's also a nationally praised Bach Fes-

tival and the Colorado Dance Festival. Every summer the Chautauqua Auditorium sponsors a very popular film series, as well as dance, music, and dramatic presentations. The list of festivals, musical productions, expositions, and dramas is far too long to be presented here. It seems there's not a day in the year without two or more choices of interesting activities going on.

Boulder Climate

	Jan.	April	July	Oct.	Average Annual Rain	Snow
Daily Highs	45°	61°	86°	66°	15"	43"
Daily Lows	20°	35°	60°	33°		

For more information contact Boulder Chamber of Commerce, 2440 Pearl Street, Boulder, CO 80302; (303) 442-1044; www.boulderchamber.com.

BOWLING GREEN, KENTUCKY

Kentucky is particularly attractive for midwestern and northern retirees who see advantages in relocating close to their prior homes, in inexpensive, low-crime surroundings. The relatively mild, four-season weather easily satisfies requirements for those who insist on colorful autumns, invigorating winters, and glorious springs.

About an hour's drive north of Nashville is the delightful little city of Bowling Green,

The more inexpensive neighborhoods in college towns also are popular with students. If you should buy or rent a home next door to a fraternity house or other student housing, you might find yourself serenaded twenty-four hours a day by full-tilt music emanating from monster speakers at a decibel level that routinely peels the paint from automobiles as they drive by.

whose year-round population of 45,000 is augmented by a student population of 15,000. Because this is the only town between Louisville and Nashville where cocktails can be served, Bowling Green's better-quality restaurants attract folks from many miles around. According to the local chamber of commerce, Bowling Green has more restaurants per capita than any other U.S. city except San Francisco.

Bowling Green looks exactly as one imagines Kentucky should look. The surrounding countryside is green, with lush rolling meadows surrounded by white fences and thoroughbred horses munching away at the Kentucky bluegrass. Because of its location, Bowling Green serves as a regional hub for retail shopping and medical services. Bowling Green University maintains a symphony orchestra and two theater groups, and it hosts frequent visits from touring artists and entertainers. The university is a major economic factor here, but so is the General Motors Corvette factory—the only Corvette production facility in the nation.

Bowling Green is one of Kentucky's larger towns but it doesn't suffer from big-city problems. Crime rates are exceptionally low, and pollution is all but nonexistent. The cost of living is 7 percent below the national average, with homes selling for 8 to 10 percent below average and utility costs at 6 percent below national averages.

Bowling Green Climate

	Jan.	April	July	Oct.	Average Annual Rain	Snow
Daily Highs	40°	66°	86°	68°	46"	16"
Daily Lows	23°	44°	66°	46°		

For more information contact Bowling Green Chamber of Commerce, 812 State Street, Bowling Green, KY 42102; (270) 781–3200; www.bgchamber.com.

CEDAR CITY, UTAH

The small college town of Cedar City (pop. 21,000) is located in the foothills of southwestern Utah, a little more than three hours by Interstate 15 from either Las Vegas or Salt Lake City. It sits in a transition zone between desert and mountain environments, and its mile-high elevation provides a cool, dry climate. Cedar City offers a wide variety of outdoor activity, and not far away are some of the most spectacular landscapes in the world. Thirty-five minutes from town, at an altitude of 5,800 feet, Brian Head Ski Resort offers excellent skiing, with powder snow usually lasting until April.

Cedar City itself usually receives four good snowfalls every winter, but warm afternoons and plenty of sunshine make quick work of melting it away. Golf is a game that can be played most of the year, even in January and February. For these reasons, Cedar City has acquired a reputation as a good place for active retirees to relocate.

Cedar City is home to Southern Utah University, with an enrollment of 6,000 students, which serves as an important center for advanced learning and public service. The school hosts numerous plays, lectures, operas, and musicals, as well as athletic events open to the public. In summer and fall, people from all over the region visit to enjoy the school's award-winning Shakespearean Festivals.

Unlike some other parts of Utah, Cedar City has a mix of different people and cultures. This population heterogeneity is partly due to workers moving into the community with manufacturing companies that have relocated here, as well as university and faculty members hired from out of state. Cedar City offers a low cost of living, usually about 10 percent below its sister city of St. George. Housing costs are dramatically lower as well.

CLOSE-UP
Checking Out College Towns

Besides the usual amenities such as climate, cost of living, housing, and proximity to large cities, you need to consider some additional points when evaluating college towns for relocation:

1. The town should not be so large that the general population overwhelms the college and dilutes its influence on the community.
2. Ideally, the campus is not far from the town center. If the school is located away from the town itself, it will be isolated and have little impact on the town's cultural and entertainment life.
3. Does the school actively reach out to the community? Some schools don't bother because they are basically technical or religious schools.
4. Does the school invite the community to participate in continuing education classes with either free or reduced tuition for noncredit classes for senior citizens?
5. Are school events such as sports, drama, music, and lecture forums open to the public?

Cedar City Climate

	Jan.	April	July	Oct.	Average Annual Rain	Snow
Daily Highs	42°	62°	84°	67°	15"	40"
Daily Lows	17°	33°	67°	52°		

For more information contact Cedar City Area Chamber of Commerce, 581 North Main Street, Cedar City, UT 84720; (435) 586–4484; www.chambercedarcity.org.

CHARLOTTESVILLE, VIRGINIA

This famous university town was founded and designed by Thomas Jefferson. The often imitated buildings are considered to be among the finest examples of classical American architecture. Two other early presidents of the United States made their homes here—James Madison and James Monroe. Both were large landholders, and their plantations are popular tourist attractions today.

Charlottesville's setting is typical of the Carolina midlands: miles of rolling hills checkered with grassy pastures, woods, and well-tended farms basking in the shadow of the Blue Ridge Mountains. Washington, D.C., is a little more than 100 miles away, and the state capital of Richmond is a 70-mile drive. Hiking and backpacking on the Appalachian Trail are just minutes away from town, and skiing not much farther. It's claimed that over 10,000 horses are pastured on farms outside of town. More than a dozen wineries dot the surrounding countryside.

The University of Virginia, which consistently ranks in the top ten among public universities, enhances community lifestyles as it serves as the area's hub for cultural and sporting events. Fortunately, Charlottesville's 70,000 residents aren't enough to overwhelm the university's 17,000 students, as well as a large faculty and staff who also participate in the city's economy and social life. The school offers a wide range of cultural amenities, including drama, concerts, lectures, dance, and summer opera. Many events are open to the public free of charge.

Medical care is superb here. The University of Virginia Health Sciences Center, a 651-bed hospital, and the 200-bed Martha Jefferson Hospital supply the most modern health care, yet medical costs are slightly below national averages. The overall cost of living is about 9 percent higher than average, however.

Charlottesville Climate

	Jan.	April	July	Oct.	Average Rain	Annual Snow
Daily Highs	43°	68°	88°	69°	47"	24"
Daily Lows	20°	45°	66°	48°		

For more information contact Chamber of Commerce, P.O. Box 1564, Charlottesville, VA 22902; (434) 295–3141; www.cville chamber.org.

CHICO, CALIFORNIA

Only a twenty-minute drive from tree-covered mountains and excellent fishing and hunting, and just a little farther to winter skiing, this is the site of California University at Chico. Chico is a typical Sacramento Valley town, with live oaks and huge shade trees along quiet streets on topography as flat as a table. The thing that puts Chico above most ordinary agri-culturally centered valley towns is its university and vibrant academic timbre. Like all California state universities, Chico State encourages senior-citizen participation with free and reduced tuition rates. Cultural events, such as concerts, plays, lectures, and foreign films, are plentiful and often free of charge to the general public.

For those who picture California housing to be impossibly expensive (and there are locations that are expensive), the university town of Chico may come as a surprise. The median sales price of homes is $10,000 below national averages, and

homes in quite acceptable neighborhoods sell for $90,000. Many good home buys in Chico are found in older neighborhoods and in some more recent developments on the edge of town. Typical construction is frame with stucco finish, favored because of its resilience in earthquakes. (A brick building tends to crack and suffer damage; a frame house simply twists and rolls with the shaking.)

Chico weather, as in all Sacramento Valley towns, is both a blessing and a draw-back, depending on your opinion of how hot summers should be. You can find days on end with temperatures in the 100-degree range. Balance that against the warm, seldom frosty winter days with almost no snow, and Chico's weather comes out a winner. After all, when the summer gets going, that's the time for you to head to the nearby mountains for a picnic beside a cool stream or a day's prospecting and panning for gold in the Feather River. A twenty-minute drive takes you to the Feather River Canyon mountain country, where homes are hidden by huge pine trees.

Chico Climate

	Jan.	April	July	Oct.	Average Rain	Annual Snow
Daily Highs	54°	72°	95°	79°	26"	0
Daily Lows	36°	44°	61°	48°		

For more information contact Chico Chamber of Commerce, 300 Salem Street, Chico, CA 95928; (530) 891–5556 or (800) 852–8570; www.chicochamber.com.

COLUMBIA, MISSOURI

With a population of more than 70,000, Columbia is more than a college town; it's more properly called a "university city." Education is big business here, with an economy solidly based on education. Three schools—University of Missouri, Stephens

College, and Columbia College—are the largest employers, ensuring an economy with a high level of prosperity and stability.

Columbia blends the sophistication of a small city with an exciting academic environment. Kansas City and St. Louis are two-hour drives in either direction for those who can't live without major league sports or other amenities of big-city life.

Columbia usually makes *Money* magazine's list of top places to live not only because of its low cost of living but also because it is "clean and green." The city is dedicated to preserving the environment, as evidenced by its ongoing campaign to plant shade trees throughout the city. Columbia's neighborhoods show a pride of ownership with neatness, a quality seldom surpassed anywhere.

Making the decision to relocate in Columbia can be made easier by a unique chamber of commerce program. Volunteers greet visitors and take them on a "windshield tour" of the city. The volunteers drive newcomers through neighborhoods ranging from economical to deluxe, past the town's colleges, golf courses, and hospitals.

Despite the upscale appearance of several Columbia neighborhoods, housing costs can be as much as 15 percent below national averages.

Columbia Climate

	Jan.	April	July	Oct.	Average Annual Rain	Snow
Daily Highs	36°	65°	89°	68°	36"	23"
Daily Lows	19°	44°	67°	46°		

For more information contact Columbia Chamber of Commerce, P.O. Box 1016, Columbia, MO 65205; (573) 874-1132; chamber.columbia.mo.us.

CORVALLIS, OREGON

Corvallis, hometown of Oregon State University, is nestled in the heart of Oregon's lovely Willamette Valley. The weather is typical western Oregon: Summer days are

CLOSE-UP
Taking College Classes

As long as you're living in a college town, why not give continuing education a try? It's different from when you were young; this time around, you sign up for subjects you *want* to study, rather than what's required to get a degree. Most adults take the classes on a noncredit basis—no tests, no term papers, no stress. University level or adult education—it doesn't matter—this is a great way to meet people and make friends in the community. You'll find yourself among a group of lively, interesting people—just the kind of folks you would like for friends.

More than two-thirds of all colleges and universities offer reduced rates to residents and sometimes free tuition for older students. Many communities have special centers, schools, and programs tailored to older adults' needs. Students of all ages, including many retired people, are taking classes, so you won't feel out of place when you're in a setting where many students are your age or older. Many of the more interesting classes are offered in the evenings so that working people can attend. You can sign up for classes on everything from ancient philosophy to auto repair.

pleasantly warm with average July and August temperatures reaching the low eighties in the afternoons. On those rare days when the mercury climbs above ninety degrees, westerly breezes from the Pacific Ocean cool things off before nightfall, and you'll be wearing sweaters after dinner. Winter temperatures hover around the forties, and the rare snowfalls average about 6 inches per year. Despite Oregon's reputation for rain, Corvallis receives an annual rainfall of about 40 inches—less than New York, Chicago, or Miami.

Oregon State University is the largest and oldest institution of higher learning in Oregon, with more than 7,000 faculty and a student body of 19,000. The town's population is about 50,000, striking just the right balance between residents and students. The university is one of the area's major employers, along with several advanced technology businesses that have found homes in Corvallis. One of the largest is Hewlett-Packard, located on a 174-acre campus, which employs about 4,000 workers. Other high-technology firms have offices here; some are operated as satellite entities.

Corvallis sits midway between Eugene and the state capital of Salem (45 miles either direction), two hours from snow skiing, and an hour from the Pacific Ocean beaches. Outdoor recreation is plentiful in this mild four-seasons climate, with everything from mountain biking and hiking on a network of trails to river rafting and golf. Performing arts and festivals are numerous, as are galleries, antiques shopping, and wineries. In and near the city you'll find more than fifty parks and wildlife preserves.

Surprisingly, housing costs here are above national averages (most Oregon cities are below the norm). This is reflected in the high-quality neighborhoods around

the city. Oregon has no sales taxes, but it manages to make up the difference with property taxes.

Corvallis Climate

	Jan.	April	July	Oct.	Average Annual Rain	Snow
Daily Highs	46°	60°	82°	65°	40"	6"
Daily Lows	33°	37°	53°	44°		

For more information contact Corvallis Area Chamber of Commerce, 420 Northwest Second Street, Corvallis, OR 97330; (541) 757-1505; www.corvallischamber.com.

FAYETTEVILLE, ARKANSAS

Fayetteville is a college town that regularly receives favorable publicity as a comfortable place to live. Located in the foothills of the Ozark Mountains, with forests, lakes, and streams nearby, Fayetteville is a progressive community with the sophistication and resources of a much larger city, yet with a comfortable, hometown feeling. This northwest corner of Arkansas is the fastest-growing region of the state, posting a population gain of 25 percent since the 1990 census, bringing the population up to 58,000, plus almost 15,000 students at the University of Arkansas.

This part of Arkansas has some of the most beautiful Ozarks scenery in the entire region, starting just a few miles from downtown Fayetteville. In the foothills is Beaver Lake, with 28,000 acres of fishing and boating and quality homes along the shores. Just minutes from the city you'll find sparkling lakes for fishing, swimming, and boating. The nearby mountains encourage hiking, camping, spelunking, and outdoor activities for all ages and physical capabilities.

The university is highly regarded and is known for the number of chief executives produced for major U.S. companies. There's also a respected school of law (Bill Clinton taught law at the university before he entered politics) and a medical school within the university. The university is the city's heart and soul, with students and faculty adding excitement and vigor to the community. To enjoy the flavor of Fayetteville's historic downtown and its campus area, visit Dickson Street, a colorful, entertaining thoroughfare filled with bistros, restaurants, and art galleries. It is reminiscent of Pearl Street in Boulder, Colorado. The nearby town of Rogers is the home of Northwest Arkansas Community College, with 2,600 students to add to the educational scene.

Housing, as you might imagine, is at Arkansas economic levels. Some historic homes in the downtown center are somewhat pricey, but not far away from the campus, homes sell for about 25 percent below national averages. A full-featured country club development is in nearby Bella Vista, built on 36,000 acres of Ozark foothills, with seven golf courses, four country clubs, tennis courts, and all the usual amenities found in developments of this nature.

Fayetteville Climate

	Jan.	April	July	Oct.	Average Annual Rain	Snow
Daily Highs	45°	69°	89°	71°	44"	6"
Daily Lows	23°	46°	68°	47°		

For more information contact Fayetteville Chamber of Commerce, 123 West Mountain, Fayetteville, AR 72702-4216; (479) 521-5776; www.fayettevillear.com.

GAINESVILLE, FLORIDA

Were it not for an occasional palm tree, Gainesville could easily be mistaken for a college town anywhere in the Midwest. Somehow, it doesn't really look like you're in Florida. Because of the University of Florida's influence, a stroll through down-

town will confirm that this is indeed a college town. Old-fashioned residential areas with tree-shaded streets justify Gainesville's official nickname, "The Tree City." Just a few minutes' driving time takes you to the country past horse farms, gated communities, and lakes.

Gainesville is a culturally stimulating city of 96,000, in addition to the school's 35,000 students. You needn't be a student to participate in the many activities connected with the university. A cultural complex with museums of art and natural history and a performing arts center serve the public at large. There also is an excellent two-year college that accepts most students over age sixty tuition-free. The extensive curriculum covers classes such as dog training, computers, and antiques collecting.

Outdoors people have plenty of recreational choices. A dozen nearby lakes invite anglers. Golf and tennis facilities abound, and beach fun at either the Gulf of Mexico or the Atlantic Ocean is a short drive away. The closest saltwater fishing is in Cedar Key, a 49-mile drive to the Gulf. Although the days are very warm in the summer, temperatures generally dip ten to twenty degrees at night. Winter can have short but stimulating cold spells, and the seasons change. In spring the dogwoods are spectacular.

Housing in Gainesville is affordable and below national averages, with a wide range of living options from expensive homes to affordable bungalows and mobile homes situated on acre-size lots. If a town of 96,000 is too large for you, nearby communities of High Springs and Archer are a fifteen-minute drive away. Housing costs are lower in those towns, and small farms are affordable.

Gainesville Climate

	Jan.	April	July	Oct.	Average Annual Rain	Snow
Daily Highs	67°	81°	91°	81°	52"	0
Daily Lows	42°	55°	71°	59°		

For more information contact Gainesville Area Chamber of Commerce, 300 East University Avenue, Suite 100, Gainesville, FL 32601; (352) 334-7100; www.gainesville chamber.com.

OXFORD, MISSISSIPPI

Oxford heads our list of favorite university towns, a place where we can imagine ourselves living. Set in the forested hills of northern Mississippi, Oxford is the model of a gracious university town in the Old South. The town is filled with stately antebellum mansions, enormous live oaks and magnolia trees, and an ancient courthouse with the obligatory statue of a Confederate soldier in the town square. It's a surprisingly small place, with a resident population of only 13,000—plus 10,000 students from the University of Mississippi. Yet the surrounding residential districts add enough people to make Oxford's business district sufficiently healthy to provide quality services suitable to a town double the size. The community is small enough that you'll meet friends just about every time you go to the supermarket or walk to the library.

A nice mixture of Yankee and southern natives adds spice to the flavor of living here. If you're not from the South, you won't be a stranger because your neighbors come from everywhere in the world. The university lures intellectuals from all over, creating an air of sophistication unknown in most isolated southern towns. What makes Oxford different from similar antebellum towns throughout the South is its cosmopolitan collection of people, attracted here by the world-famous university. Oxford is famous as a writer's mecca. Novelists John Grisham, Larry Brown, Cynthia Shearer, and Barry Hannah have homes here, but the most famous of the local writers is, of course, William Faulkner.

Retirees find Oxford a wonderful place for continuing education; people over the age of 55 can take three hours of classes tuition-free per semester and can audit as many classes as they care to. The school is deeply connected with the community, inviting local residents to join in many programs of sports and culture.

Although upscale homes have soared in value in the past few years, there are plenty of affordable neighborhoods with inexpensive prices and rents. Average housing prices, while far above ordinary Mississippi communities, are usually at least 10 percent below national averages.

Oxford Climate

	Jan.	April	July	Oct.	Average Annual Rain	Snow
Daily Highs	51°	75°	93°	76°	56"	5"
Daily Lows	31°	50°	69°	49°		

For more information contact Oxford-Lafayette County Chamber of Commerce, P.O. Box 147, Oxford, MS 38655; (662) 234-4651; chamber.oxfordms.com.

VALDOSTA, GEORGIA

In their mad rush to get to Florida for vacations, many travelers zip past Valdosta (pop. 44,000), never suspecting that a delightful little city sits undiscovered just off Interstate 75. Some tourists may stay overnight in a motel, perhaps do some shopping at the manufacturers' outlet stores, then wheel their cars back onto the Interstate to resume the high-speed parade to the saltwater beaches a couple of hours down the road.

Valdosta is set in Georgia's historic Plantation Trace, a region marked by fertile plains, bountiful woods, and hundreds of blue lakes. Valdosta is proud of its Victorian architecture as well as modern subdivisions featuring immaculately maintained neighborhoods shaded by enormous trees and enhanced by landscaping that emphasizes flowering plants.

Valdosta State University's grounds and campus are in keeping with the upscale look of its surroundings. The school consists of two campuses, totaling 200 acres, located about a mile apart. The university offers continuing education, with low cost fees, in classes ranging from calligraphy to tai chi.

The cost of living in Valdosta is less than the national average, with housing costs ranging from 10 to 15 percent below the norm. The region benefits from a recession-resistant economy based on military and university payrolls, which don't vary a great deal. Moody Air Force Base employs 4,700 civilians, and the university hires 2,200 local residents. Because of a high turnover of Air Force families (mostly officers) who are transferred in and out for training, there are plenty of apartment complexes scattered about town. The quality real estate we have looked at here is bargain-priced, with the median sales about 10 percent below national averages.

Valdosta Climate

	Jan.	April	July	Oct.	Average Annual Rain	Average Annual Snow
Daily Highs	70°	80°	94°	83°	49"	0
Daily Lows	45°	54°	71°	59°		

For more information contact Valdosta Chamber of Commerce, 416 North Ashley Street, Valdosta, GA 31603; (229) 247-8100; www.valdostachamber.com.

RELOCATING IN THE WEST

Most of the country's fastest-growing towns and cities are located out West. This is where some of the more favorable job markets are found, as well as some of the more popular retirement destinations. Some of the major centers of high technology sprang up in the West to spread across the continent. The West is still where new high-tech innovations begin and where many aerospace, computer, and manufacturing jobs originate. If you are looking for employment, you might consider looking in this region. If you are seeking unusual weather and awesome scenery, you can't go too far wrong with looking West.

The range of climates and scenic attractions found in the western states is almost bewildering—from snow-clad mountains and open sky country of Montana and Idaho to the Great Salt Lake Desert, from the Grand Canyon to tall pine forests of the Rocky Mountains and the enormous metropolis of Phoenix. In the West you'll find Mount Whitney, the highest mountain peak in the contiguous continental United States, with an elevation at the summit 14,491 feet above sea level; less than 150 miles away is the lowest elevation in the Western Hemisphere—Death Valley, which hunkers down at 282 feet below sea level. From southern California's semitropical climate of sunshine and surf to Sierra Mountain ski resorts—just about any kind of outdoor recreation imaginable is waiting for you. North America's only rain forests are on Washington's Olympic Peninsula, which contrast with expanses of arid deserts in California, Arizona, and Nevada. As if this weren't enough, the Pacific Coast has some of the most beautiful and uncluttered seascapes in the world.

Following are some relocation suggestions, based on our research. We try to consider economic conditions in each city, as well as the scenic and esthetic values, climate, and livability. Most places listed have enjoyed good track records for job and business growth. All communities listed are appropriate for retirees who are considering relocation.

ALBUQUERQUE, NEW MEXICO

Albuquerque is routinely recommended by travel and retirement writers as a place for a new beginning. It enjoys a unique climate due to its 5,000-foot altitude, dry air, and mild weather. Because of low humidity, the regional weather feels milder than weather charts might suggest. In July, the hottest month, daytime temperatures usually top out in the low nineties, and then you'll find a sweater comfortable that same evening. Because of the altitude, it does snow in the winter—usually no more than 1 or 2 inches at a time—but because even the coldest winter days in Albuquerque usually reach fifty degrees by afternoon, snow doesn't stick around for long.

Albuquerque is the metropolitan hub of New Mexico and one of the major high-technology centers of the Southwest. As such, it attracts people from all over the country to work and retire. The economy has been robust, resulting in a gain of 21 percent in population over the past decade, approaching a half million inhabitants. Growth has been graceful, with attractive residential neighborhoods mixing traditional ranch-style homes with pueblo-adobe themes. Nearby communities of new homes, such as Rio Rancho, make commuting an easy task.

Albuquerque's downtown section is clean, modern, prosperous looking, polished, and tastefully designed. A pedestrian mall completes the picture of a pleasant city center. The city has taken pains to preserve its historic sector. Preservation was possible partly because the coming of the railroad in 1880 moved the downtown area away from the original plaza, thus sparing it from development. Today that area, now known as Old Town, offers interesting restaurants and shops and maintains the historic flavor of the Old West.

The University of New Mexico is too small to have an enormous impact on the social and cultural life of such a large city, but from our perspective, some of the most desirable neighborhoods are those near the campus, in the southern part of the city (east of downtown). These neighborhoods are typical of the many pleasant, livable areas in and around Albuquerque. Mature trees shade the streets, and most homes are of brick-and-frame construction.

The community of Rio Rancho is a typical Albuquerque commuter and retirement development, tucked away from city congestion, just twenty minutes from downtown and forty-five minutes from Santa Fe. The development started some years ago as a scheme to sell parcels of worthless desert landscape to out-of-state retirees. Rio Rancho targeted New Yorkers, and as a result,

many residents come from that state. Local people were skeptical about the project but were surprised when it actually took off, and it hasn't stopped since. Rio Rancho's population almost doubled over the past ten years, with 52,000 people now living on ranch land that twenty-five years ago supported about 200 cows. With a twenty-seven-hole golf course and a panorama of the Sandia Mountains in the distance, Rio Rancho is a blend of Southwest desert and middle-class suburb.

Albuquerque Climate

	Jan.	April	July	Oct.	Average Annual Rain	Snow
Daily Highs	47°	71°	92°	72°	8"	12"
Daily Lows	22°	40°	64°	43°		

For more information contact Greater Albuquerque Chamber of Commerce, 401 Second Street N.W., Albuquerque, NM 87102; (505) 764-3700; www.gacc.org; or Rio Rancho Chamber of Commerce, 1781 Rio Rancho Drive, Rio Rancho, NM 87124; (505) 892-1533; www.rrchamber.org.

AUSTIN, TEXAS

Another fast-growing center of high-tech industry and blossoming business, the Austin metro area has seen a population growth of 41 percent since the 1990 census, with the city of Austin posting a 13 percent gain to its present population of 656,000. Austin's high-tech sector has been growing at a rate of 7 percent a year. Over the past ten years, a number of advanced technology companies have moved or started up here, creating about 100,000 jobs. Some major employers are Dell, Motorola, and IBM. The University of Texas and the city of Austin account for more than 30,000 jobs between them.

Most Texas cities spread out on flat landscapes, but Austin sits on the fringe of the Texas Hill Country, built on a series of gentle hills. Austin is the capital of Texas; the downtown's centerpiece is the state capitol building, with its extensive grounds and park-like landscaping. The building is worth a visit just to see the marvelous workmanship in rose-colored granite. The downtown displays an interesting mixture of modern buildings and older ones, creating an air of informality.

Austin has gained fame as a music center, with country and western music, jazz, and reggae heard in the clubs around the city, particularly on Sixth Street, the city's renovated nineteenth-century historic district. Museums, theaters, and art galleries are well attended throughout the city. A symphony, ballet, and lyric opera complement the cultural offerings.

Much too large to be considered a college town, Austin nevertheless is proud of its University of Texas campus, with its exceptional libraries, museums, sports activities, and cultural facilities. The LBJ Library is located on the university campus. There's also a community college offering continuing education and personal development courses of interest to senior citizens.

Austin is circled with suburbs convenient for commuters and retirees. One we like is Georgetown, an interesting town that is proud of its place in history and of its wealth of Victorian architecture. The town's focal point is a historic Courthouse Square, complete with antiques stores and boutiques. The town government is quite active in the restoration and preservation of this historic district, with 180 homes and commercial structures designated as having historical significance. Some are in use as restaurants and bed-and-breakfasts. One of Del Webb's Sun City master-planned retirement centers is located nearby, on a 5,300-acre tract. Designed for the fifty-and-older crowd, this is a typical Del Webb residential development featuring the usual golf courses, lighted tennis courts, biking trails, and all the trappings of an active retirement village.

Only 27 miles from Austin by Interstate 35, Georgetown is clearly within easy commuting distance. This makes it convenient for residents to enjoy Austin's big-city amenities such as shopping, sports events, and entertainment. The cost of living in the Austin area is right at or slightly above national averages. Housing costs, at the time of writing, are about 7 percent above average.

Austin Climate

	Jan.	Apr.	July	Oct.	Average Annual Rain	Snow
Daily Highs	59°	79°	95°	81°	32"	1"
Daily Lows	39°	58°	74°	59°		

For more information contact Greater Austin Chamber of Commerce, P.O. Box 1967, Austin, TX 78767; (512) 478–9383; www.austin-chamber.org.

DENVER, COLORADO

Another western metropolitan area with a phenomenal growth record, Denver posted a 30 percent increase in population in the 1990s. Denver's population of more than a half million—counting suburbs and nearby towns, it's more than two and a half million—makes it the largest city within a radius of 600 miles.

Starting out as a mining camp when a few gold nuggets were discovered in a creek in 1858, Denver's gold turned the small mining camp into a city almost overnight. Today, Denver's gold mining economy has been replaced by major telecommunications companies and a variety of other high-tech industries, many located in Denver's downtown section.

Denver is a clean city with pleasant, tree-shaded residential areas and an abundance of affordable, quality apartment buildings. Most homes are built of brick, especially older ones. According to a local legend, an early-day mayor owned a brick factory, so he pushed for a law ordering all homes to be constructed of brick. Maybe it's not true, but the brick construction does add a special touch to Denver's architectural flavor.

The city of Denver has several top-quality and very livable neighborhoods, but also several low-cost districts that cause some people to feel uncomfortable. Most newcomers will probably elect to relocate in one of the many suburbs that surround the city, all within easy commuting distance, such as Aurora and Littleton. In fact, just about anywhere on Denver's perimeter can be recommended as safe, comfortable places to live. From there, it's an easy trip downtown for work, shopping, theater, or cultural events.

Denver seems to be up to its waist in professional sports. Professional teams calling Denver their hometown are the Denver Broncos (football), the Denver Nuggets (basketball), the Colorado Avalanche (hockey), the Colorado Rapids (soccer), and the Colorado Rockies (baseball).

Denver's high elevation and unique local weather patterns make winters here rather interesting, with an average yearly snowfall of 60 inches. From time to time, television newscasts depict Denver's airport buried under banks of drifting snow, with airplanes grounded and passengers stranded in the terminal. Yet it isn't as bad as it appears. People here are used to snowfalls of a foot or more overnight, and they can deal with it. They know that when they wake up to see several inches of snow, there's a good chance that by noon the city will be basking in warm sunshine, and the snow doesn't have a chance. Denver enjoys an average of 300 sunny days a year, and golf courses are always open for

play. There can be as many as thirty playing days in the month of January.

Denver Climate

	Jan.	April	July	Oct.	Average Annual Rain	Snow
Daily Highs	43°	61°	88°	67°	15"	60"
Daily Lows	16°	34°	59°	37°		

For more information contact Denver Chamber of Commerce, 1445 Market Street, Denver CO 80202-1729; (303) 534-8500; www.denverchamber.org.

PHOENIX, ARIZONA

High-tech and aerospace companies are significant employers in the Phoenix area. Some well-known companies represented are Intel, Boeing, Motorola, and Allied Signal Corp. About 8,000 people work for American Express in its Phoenix facility. While high tech is the largest growth sector in Phoenix, tourism also is important, with a reputed 250,000 people employed directly or indirectly in the tourism industry.

Phoenix is an astonishing large, sprawling conglomerate of communities. In the 1990s alone more than a million new residents relocated in the Phoenix area, swelling the population to 3,200,000 inhabitants, 1,300,000 of them within Phoenix's city limits.

The city of Phoenix is a great place to work but not necessarily the best place to live. When people speak of "relocating in Phoenix," they usually mean any one of a dozen communities on the expanding fringes of the metro area—places such as Mesa, Tempe, and Scottsdale. The largest expansions are in the Del Webb Sun City developments.

Until a few years ago, Scottsdale was separated from Phoenix by miles of open desert. Today you can't tell when you've left one city and entered another unless you happen to see a city limits sign. Scottsdale has always been a symbol of elegant and luxury living. Beautifully landscaped boulevards are lined with so many fabulous, prestige-name stores that your credit card vibrates as you drive past. Sumptuous residential neighborhoods display homes so artistic and palatial that you'll hate yourself for not being able to afford one. However, even though Scottsdale is synonymous with expensive living, it's still possible to find a few neighborhoods where housing costs aren't much higher than in the older Sun City neighborhoods. These are the exceptions, of course. Overall, the cost of Scottsdale real estate is a whopping 33 to 38 percent above national averages. The nearby communities of Cave Creek and Carefree are even more upscale, with absolutely gorgeous desert settings. At a slightly higher elevation than Phoenix, Cave Creek and Carefree enjoy a climate considerably cooler than Phoenix. If you can afford it, it is truly worth living here.

On the eastern edge of Phoenix, the rapidly growing community of Apache Junction represents a more affordable example for retirement or commuting. The area doesn't have the charisma or charm of Scottsdale (few places do), but real estate doesn't come with an exorbitant price tag. A thirty-minute ride via the fast-moving Superstition Freeway whisks you to downtown Phoenix or to Sky Harbor Airport. Apache Junction can almost claim rural status due to its position on the border between the city and open country. In the distance the Superstition Mountains rise above the desert floor, presenting an ominous, fortress-like appearance.

Apache Junction has acquired a dual personality in its role as a popular retirement destination for both permanent and temporary residents. Retirees from the Midwest and East are ending their retirement search when they discover Apache Junction's laid-back attitude and the area's year-round summer. From 1990 to 2003, the permanent population doubled to about 20,000. Much of this increase can be attributed to retirees.

Apache Junction's second role in retirement is with RV enthusiasts and "snowbirds" who travel to Arizona each winter. They enjoy it here because the town welcomes them (and their money) so warmly and because the city of Phoenix is easy to visit from the town. More than forty mobile-home and RV parks accommodate some of these visitors. Their number is said to approach 35,000 for the season. Conventional housing sells for what probably are the lowest prices in the Phoenix area.

Phoenix Climate

	Jan.	April	July	Oct.	Average Annual Rain	Snow
Daily Highs	65°	83°	105°	88°	7"	0
Daily Lows	39°	53°	80°	59°		

For more information contact Greater Phoenix Chamber of Commerce, 201 North Central Avenue, Suite 2700, Phoenix, AZ 85073; (602) 254–5521; www.phoenixchamber.com.

PORTLAND, OREGON

Portland was founded on the banks of the Columbia and Williamette Rivers, where the two rivers join together, about 65 miles from the Pacific Ocean. This surprising city calls itself "the City of Roses" and is populated by friendly people surrounded by awesome beauty. Soaring evergreen trees and snow-capped mountains command the horizon. Nearby are lush green fields, gently flowing rivers, and bountiful flower gardens.

As one of the Pacific Coast's most important seaports, over the years Portland attracted an assortment of industries—everything from light manufacturing to lumber. This diverse economic base helps reduce the effect of an adverse economy. In the 1990s the city evolved into a major high-tech center, with an estimated 1,200 high-tech companies employing some 64,000 workers at the peak of the high-tech boom. Many didn't survive the "dot-com" bust, but the failures are overshadowed by successful companies such as Hewlett-Packard, Intel, Epson, and NEC, all of which have plants in the Portland area. The Portland area accounts for 86 percent of Oregon's technology employment and almost one-fifth of the state's total manufacturing jobs. This makes the area especially popular with older computer and Internet specialists who are looking at retirement before long.

Portland has an undeserved reputation for excessively rainy weather. The fact is, Portland receives much less rain than most cities in the eastern regions of the United States—less than 40 inches (compared with Miami's 60 inches, or nearby Astoria, Oregon's 70 inches). Coastal Oregon just *seems* to have more rain because it comes down in long, lazy drizzles rather than in vigorous downpours. Winter rains can sometimes drag on for several days. Glorious spring, summer, and fall weather makes amends for damp winters.

Portland's location is ideal for those who love the convenience of a large city yet want access to the countryside, mountains, and seashore. A short drive in one direction takes you across the Cascade Mountains to beautiful, uncrowded Pacific beaches. Travel the other direction and you find yourself in Oregon's famous wine country, and just a little farther yet, among truly rugged mountains with lush forests and trout streams. On the other side of these mountains is fascinating high desert country with lava beds, prairies, and herds of deer and antelope.

Because of Portland's many individual-ized neighborhoods—some of them reminiscent of San Francisco's Victorian districts—many people choose to relocate in various neighborhoods in the city, near central Portland, rather than flee to the suburbs. This solves the commuting problem because they can go to work or shopping by using Portland's excellent public transportation system.

Many charming suburbs and adjoining towns surround Portland. One that stands out is Portland's sister city of Vancouver, Washington. Vancouver is reached via an impressive bridge across the broad Columbia River, a short commute to downtown Portland. Some might consider Vancouver just another of Portland's bedroom communities, but with a population of 144,000, that designation would be misleading. Vancouver's city center is lively, dynamic, and self-contained, and it has its own high-tech manufacturing, traditional industry, and businesses to provide jobs that don't require commuting. In fact, some workers commute to Vancouver from Portland.

Residential neighborhoods here tend to have homes on larger lots than similar neighborhoods in Portland, and with smaller price tags—usually about 10 percent below national averages. In the distance the startling beauty of Mount St. Helens and the challenging ski slopes of Mount Hood are just a short drive away.

One difference between Vancouver and Portland is the collection of taxes. The state of Washington does not impose a state income tax, while the state of Oregon does not collect a state sales tax. As you can imagine, both states make up for the loss of tax revenue by collecting it through property taxes. Residents of Vancouver, however, have it both ways. They pay no state taxes on income, yet by crossing over the Columbia River bridge, they can make major purchases in Oregon and avoid sales tax!

Portland Climate

	Jan.	April	July	Oct.	Average Annual Rain	Snow
Daily Highs	44°	60°	80°	64°	37"	7"
Daily Lows	34°	41°	56°	45°		

For more information contact Portland Chamber of Commerce, 520 Southwest Yamhill Street, Suite 1000, Portland, OR 97204; (503) 224-8684; www.portland alliance.org; or Greater Vancouver Chamber of Commerce, 1101 Broadway, Suite 120, Vancouver, WA 98660; (360) 694-2588; www.vancouverusa.com.

SEATTLE, WASHINGTON

Most of the state of Washington is sparsely populated, with small towns and occasional small cities scattered over flat stretches of wheat fields and sagebrush or tucked away in the Cascade Range. The most populated area is concentrated along the shores of Puget Sound, with towns and small cities stretching from Everett in the north to Olympia to the south. The combined population of this corridor is nearly two and a half million residents, ranking the Seattle metro area twentieth in terms of total population in the United States.

Seattle, of course, is the centerpiece. The setting here is beautiful, with views of the protected waters of the sound with magnificent snow-topped mountains in the background. Puget Sound moderates the climate, and a high mountain range to the west shelters the region from Pacific storms. Abundant rainfall and lack of frost results in greenness all year. Seattle's average annual rainfall of 36 inches is less than most eastern and midwestern cites receive. It usually doesn't rain hard in Seattle, but it rains often, sometimes a slow, misty drizzle. When the sun comes out, it is glorious!

Seattle is one of the Pacific Coast's major ports for transpacific and European trade. The sprawling complex of towns and small cities around Seattle has become a high-tech hub and a leading center for advanced technology in computer software, biotechnology, electronics, medical equipment, and environmental engineering.

Because we favor smaller towns and cities over large places like Seattle, we concentrated our research in the direction of smaller communities. Most people who work in Seattle or other cities in the region try to commute from their favorite smaller town, either by automobile, by ferryboat, or even by private speedboats. The list of towns is endless, with locations to suit any lifestyle and economic situation.

Seattle Climate

	Jan.	April	July	Oct.	Average Annual Rain	Snow
Daily Highs	44°	57°	75°	60°	39"	7"
Daily Lows	34°	41°	54°	45°		

For more information contact Greater Seattle Chamber of Commerce, 1301 Fifth Avenue, Suite 2400, Seattle, WA 98101-2611; (206) 389-7200; www.seattlechamber.com.

SALT LAKE CITY AND PROVO, UTAH

Salt Lake was settled in 1847, when Brigham Young led a caravan of his Mormon followers across the plains and mountains in search of freedom from religious persecution. When the travelers looked down from the Wasatch Mountains to the valley of the Great Salt Lake, they decided that this was the Promised Land where they would live. They set to work tilling the soil that same day and began transforming the arid, desolate land into today's beautiful, well-planned Salt Lake City.

At first the city's growth depended on the inflow of Mormon converts from Europe and America. Later on, industrial and business expansion brought in many non-Mormon workers. Although 69 percent of Utah's residents belong to the Church of Jesus Christ of Latter-Day Saints, Salt Lake City is much more heterogeneous. Almost half of Salt Lake City's population is now non-Mormon.

Salt Lake City, with a population of 173,000, offers clean, livable neighborhoods, with canyon hiking trails within walking distance of home. The city center surrounds the chief buildings of the Mormon Church, which is surrounded by landscaped grounds. A major landmark, Temple Square with its famous Sea Gull Monument, sits at an altitude of 4,400 feet. This elevation ensures pleasant summers, lots of sunshine, and plenty of snow in the nearby mountains for world-class skiing.

Utah's economy usually outpaces that of the nation, with Salt Lake City leading the way in its ability to attract new businesses and create jobs. This metropolitan population of around 800,000 comprises a healthy marketing area. The overall cost of living in Salt Lake City is slightly below average, helped in part by exceptionally low real estate prices, 12 percent below national averages, and utility costs 10 percent lower than average.

Salt Lake City and Provo Climate

	Jan.	Apr.	July	Oct.	Average Annual Rain	Snow
Daily Highs	37°	61°	93°	67°	15″	58″
Daily Lows	20°	37°	62°	39°		

For more information contact Salt Lake Chamber of Commerce, 175 East 400 South Street, Salt Lake City, UT 84111; (801) 364–3631; www.saltlakechamber.org; or Provo–Orem Chamber of Commerce, 51 South University Avenue, Suite 215, Provo, UT 84601; (801) 379-2555; www.thechamber.org/chamber.shtml.

SAN LUIS OBISPO, CALIFORNIA

San Luis Obispo (pop. 43,000) is another place that could be listed as a college town because it is indeed that—yet there's something special about the city that deserves more attention. As far as we are concerned, this is one of the better candidates for relocation in the state of California, certainly a hometown one could be proud of.

Situated on the coastal Highway 101, about halfway between Los Angeles and San Francisco, San Luis Obispo enjoys one of California's best climates. If you don't believe this, just take a look at the temperature chart showing the mild winters and cool summers. San Luis Obispo enjoys at least 300 days of sunshine every year. Pacific beaches are but a fifteen-minute drive from the downtown center, yet the town is protected from ocean fog and clouds by a barrier of low mountains. Large, leafy trees arch over downtown commercial avenues that are lined with prosperous businesses and stores with tastefully designed exteriors. Nationally known outlets you would expect to find only in shopping malls, including fashionable clothing stores, large drugstores, and boutiques of all description, are located right in the center of town, instead of a ten-minute drive to the strip malls on the edge of town.

San Luis Obispo is an excellent example of how a university can bolster and develop a community's economy. We remember the town from the 1960s when forced to drive through on our way to Santa Barbara. Back then it was a dreary place, a bottleneck on a slow section of Highway 101, before the present-day bypass. Some side streets were unpaved, there were no trees on the downtown streets, and the only interesting part about San Luis Obispo was the old Spanish mission that sat forlornly, almost ignored on the main drag. The city center was a disaster, studded with vacant buildings, with about half of the retail stores abandoned. The community was so unappealing, so difficult to lure people to move there, that the local school district had to create a special program to recruit teachers. The physical surroundings were attractive enough, but few job opportunities lured newcomers into the community.

Then, in the late 1960s and early 1970s, California Polytechnic State University changed from a backwater agricultural college into a full-fledged university with a curriculum that combines technical and professional endeavors with arts and humanities. As Cal Poly grew in reputation and stature, San Luis Obispo progressed with it. Today Cal Poly hosts 17,500 students on its 6,000-acre campus nestled in the foothills on the edge of the city. The college almost single-handedly provided the economic job growth necessary for the city's modern-day affluence. The change in the landscape and the livability of the city have been nothing less than dramatic.

Residential neighborhoods present enticing retirement scenarios, with nicely landscaped properties and views of mountains in the distance. Real estate prices, once at ridiculously low levels, have increased considerably over the past few years, as the real estate market climbed along with other quality California communities. Several beach communities are just minutes away from town, some with gorgeous views of the ocean, others featuring surfing and clamming just blocks from their homes.

San Luis Obispo Climate

	Jan.	April	July	Oct.	Average Annual Rain	Snow
Daily Highs	64°	67°	73°	74°	12"	0
Daily Lows	48°	42°	53°	48°		

For more information contact Chamber of Commerce of San Luis Obispo, 1039 Chorro Street, San Luis Obispo, CA 93401; (805) 781-2777; www.slochamber.org.

RELOCATING IN THE EAST

Many people from the Midwest and East prefer to remain east of the Mississippi so they won't be so far away from their origins, friends, and family. When relocating voluntarily, they try to find new hometowns in pleasant communities where they can reasonably expect occasional visits from family and friends, or where they can conveniently return to their old stomping grounds from time to time. Florida and the eastern seaboard states are popular relocation destinations because friends are more likely to stop in and visit on their way to the annual Florida vacation than if the new hometown were isolated clear across the continent. Other people look fondly on the mild winters in the southern parts of the country, particularly in the states where active campaigns for attracting newcomers are in process. Often, factories and businesses move lock, stock, and barrel from the North to one of the lower-wage states in the South or Southeast. This creates another reason to relocate: to be near the runaway industry and claim your job back.

Following are a few of our favorites, places we've investigated and found to be viable choices for relocation, communities where we would personally feel comfortable living.

AMHERST, MASSACHUSETTS

Amherst is one of several charming towns located in the beautiful Pioneer Valley, one of the first inland regions settled by early colonists who used the Connecticut River for travel and commerce from Long Island Sound north into Canada. The fertile valley is framed with ancient mountains of the Hadley range, now eroded into impressive hills, and endowed with farms, forests, and traditional New England villages. Boston is two hours away, and it's three and a half hours to New York City. Yet everything one really needs can be found right here; the combined population of nearby communities forms a sizable consumer market without creating a large-city environment. Residents claim some of the local restaurants rival anything New York has to offer.

The classically historic town center of Amherst features a spacious town common, lined with trees and the obligatory statues and monuments. You can stroll past the home where Emily Dickinson was born and raised, where poet Robert Frost lived and where he taught, and where Eugene Field composed his first poem. Noah Webster, famous for his dictionary, resided in Amherst and helped found Amherst College, one of three small schools here with large reputations.

In all, five institutions of higher learning are found among the towns of Amherst, Northampton, and Hadley. These five colleges contribute to an exciting and fascinating cultural lifestyle, with frequent free lectures, museums, galleries, and film and theater events. Northampton, the home of the University of Massachusetts, 15 minutes from Amherst, was nominated "best small arts town in the United States" in a recent issue of a national magazine. The university's Fine Arts Center brings major performing artists to the community, and Broadway productions are staged by another company.

The climate here is typical New England, with plenty of rain in the summer as well as generous snowfalls in the winter. We visited in the middle of May, and we woke up one morning to a dazzling display of snow on the ground, frosting the evergreens, making a scene worthy of a Currier and Ives painting. Actually less than an inch of snow had fallen; later that day, the temperatures were in the low seventies.

Real estate in Amherst, Northampton, and to a lesser degree the surrounding areas is booming. Values continue to rise as affluent people retire here and build expensive homes. However, bargains are still to be found in the outlying areas, in places like Williamsburg to the north. A couple we interviewed who relocated from New York solved their real estate needs by buying forty acres of wooded land between Amherst and Belchertown—about fifteen minutes from town—then they installed their own well, brought in electricity, and had a home built in the middle of the acreage, for complete quiet and privacy, a 180-degree change from crowded Manhattan.

Amherst Climate

	Jan.	April	July	Oct.	Average Annual Rain	Snow
Daily Highs	35°	60°	84°	65°	43"	41"
Daily Lows	12°	34°	61°	38°		

For more information contact Amherst Area Chamber of Commerce, 409 Main Street, Amherst, MA 01002; (413) 253-0700; www.amherstarea.com.

BIRMINGHAM, ALABAMA

Alabama is one of the most active states when it comes to encouraging retirees and businesses to relocate. These efforts have been successful in bringing in several large businesses and industrial plants, creating job opportunities as well as relocating hundreds of retired couples.

One of the advantages to relocating in Alabama is an extremely low property tax rate. In the towns we researched, taxes on a home worth $150,000 were typically around $600 a year, compared with a similar home in Florida, which would be taxed at $2,700 a year. Other taxes follow a similar pattern. Also, the $150,000 will buy a surprisingly high-quality home.

Birmingham is Alabama's largest city and the center of a large industrial and technical complex that employs many skilled technical and executive workers. With a population of about 250,000, plus at least twice that many in the surrounding communities, many newcomers decide to live in one of the many quality suburbs that ring Birmingham rather than in the city itself. These communities are surrounded by forested hills, protected greenbelts, and several lakes. On Birmingham's southern flank, particularly, the hustle and bustle of a large population center fades away into quiet suburbs and finally disappears into a countrylike setting. It's not exactly country, because you are within a half-hour drive of downtown Birmingham, with all its cultural and commercial amenities.

Our favorite relocation choice here is Pelham, with a population of 15,000. The nearby suburb of Hoover is of similar size and is also desirable as a place to live. Many new developments are hidden in woodlands, with homes on large, wooded lots. The average price of homes sold here is almost double that of most other Alabama communities. That says something for the quality and amenities.

For a much less expensive alternative in the Birmingham area, there is the city of Jasper, about a half hour north of the city via an expressway. Because of a shift in the economy when the primary industry of coal production ceased, the community has been very active in recruiting newcomers as an economic development activity. Located in an area of lakes and rivers where golf, hunting, and fishing can be enjoyed year-round, Jasper offers a totally different lifestyle from the more formal suburbs to the south of Birmingham. Some truly nice developments can be found on the shore of a 35-mile-long lake just outside of town. Commuting time to Birmingham is about forty-five minutes at the moment, but when a new expressway is completed, the drive will take about thirty minutes.

Birmingham Climate

	Jan.	April	July	Oct.	Average Annual Rain	Snow
Daily Highs	52°	75°	91°	74°	52"	2"
Daily Lows	33°	51°	70°	51°		

For more information contact Birmingham Regional Chamber of Commerce, 505 Twentieth Street North, Birmingham, AL 35203; (205) 324–2100; www.birmingham chamber.com; or Pelham Chamber of Commerce, P.O. Box 324, Pelham, AL 35124; (205) 663–4542; www.shelbychamber.org; or Jasper Chamber of Commerce, 400 West Nineteenth Street, Jasper, AL 35502-1589; www.jaspercity.com.

COLUMBIA, SOUTH CAROLINA

Most Old South cities grew haphazardly, with roads and streets going in random directions, without planning of any sort. But Columbia is different; it was carefully thought out. Settled by the British in the early 1700s, Columbia was selected to be

the site of South Carolina's new state capital in 1786. This was South Carolina's first planned city, with wide streets arranged in a grid pattern, and the second planned city in the United States (Savannah, Georgia, being the first). Robert Mills, one of the pioneers of American architecture, designed several buildings in Columbia, as well as many in Washington, D.C. (one of his more famous works is the Washington Monument).

Columbia is strategically located in the heart of South Carolina, with the mountains and ocean each a little more than a two-hour drive in either direction. At the western edge of the city, rolling foothills head toward the Blue Ridge Mountains; to the east, the country is flat all the way to the Atlantic Ocean. Only a short drive from downtown Columbia is a 50,000-acre lake covering an area of 78 square miles, with 659 miles of shoreline. Lake Murray offers boating, sailing, canoeing, fishing, skiing, swimming, and camping.

Columbia combines the charm of a rich past with the vibrancy of the emerging sunbelt economy, a center for military, academics, government, and business. With a population of 118,000, Columbia is South Carolina's most populous city, yet it doesn't have the feeling of a big city. A surprising number of northerners have found this to be a great place for retirement.

Columbia is an educational center of the region, with the University of South Carolina as a focal point. The university, with 28,000 students, is a major source of cultural enrichment that attracts academics from around the nation, many of whom later join the growing ranks of Columbia's retirees. This is a comfortable city, with the vast majority of the housing owner-occupied. The streets are shaded with large trees, and there's a quiet charm that comes with ordinary people living in ordinary neighborhoods. Yet Columbia has its sophisticated side as well, with a cosmopolitan ambience that goes with being a university town. The cost of living is very favorable here, with housing typically selling about 7 to 10 percent below national averages.

Columbia Climate

	Jan.	April	July	Oct.	Average Annual Rain	Snow
Daily Highs	56°	77°	92°	77°	49"	2"
Daily Lows	33°	51°	70°	50°		

For more information contact South Carolina Chamber of Commerce, 1201 Main Street, Suite 1810, Columbia, SC 29201; (800) 799–4601; www.sccc.org.

GULFPORT AND BILOXI, MISSISSIPPI

Before we started our research into relocation in the state of Mississippi, we were burdened by stereotypes of what the South was probably like. We were in for one of our more pleasant surprises. We found a friendly and welcoming climate throughout all of the communities we visited, a gracious mixture of modern and old-fashioned southern traditions. Winters are mild, the cost of living is low, and taxes are reasonable.

Mississippi is one of the pioneers in retirement attraction programs, with a generous budget for advertising and organizing welcoming committees in individual communities that have become adroit at rolling out the welcome mat.

One of our biggest surprises came when we researched the Gulfport–Biloxi stretch of Mississippi's Gulf Coast. The region has undergone a remarkable economic boom that doesn't seem to want to quit. A dramatic expansion of Las Vegas–style gambling casinos has been the sparkplug of an economic explosion that created thousands of jobs and changed the face of the community forever. Gambling's boost to the local economy changed the environment from a string of small fishing and summer tourist towns to a healthy, year-round business cycle, with casinos as the catalyst. Retirees are flocking here as well as job seekers because casinos have a way of creating lots of part-time work—just the ticket for retirees.

Although you might find acceptable neighborhoods near the casino strip, we believe the best bets for relocation here are in the smaller towns that line the beach on either side of the Gulfport–Biloxi complex. The quiet and peaceful atmosphere of places like Pass Christian, Long Beach, and Bay St. Louis come to mind. As one resident of Pass Christian said, "Here we have 26 miles of quiet beach all to ourselves, away from the crowded and honky-tonk gambling strip." A bonus to living in small communities, away from the gambling, is an exceptionally low crime rate, just as you would expect in other Mississippi towns—according to FBI statistics, among the lowest in the country.

Real estate prices in these small towns are higher than in most Mississippi locations—no surprise in that—yet those moving in from other parts of the country are impressed by values offered on new housing and on Victorian homes in peaceful neighborhoods.

Some local residents complain about the vastly increased number of tourists who visit here, and many grumble about the increased automobile traffic. Yet were it not for the casinos and the crowds of tourists, there would not be the first-class facilities available to all, such as quality golf courses, excellent restaurants, and world-class shopping.

Gulfport and Biloxi Climate

	Jan.	April	July	Oct.	Average Annual Rain	Snow
Daily Highs	61°	77°	90°	79°	61"	0
Daily Lows	49°	60°	74°	66°		

For more information contact Biloxi Chamber of Commerce, 1048 Beach Boulevard, Biloxi, MS 39533; (228) 374-2717; www.mscoastchamber.com.

FORT MYERS, FLORIDA

Fort Myers, on Florida's west coast, was an early-day "discovery" by Henry Ford and his friend Thomas Edison, who both maintained winter homes there. Edison loved to experiment with trees and shrubs, particularly palm trees, and he was responsible for some of the city's interesting landscaping by financing the planting of the streets with exotic greenery. It's claimed that over 70 varieties of palms grace the streets of Fort Myers thanks to Edison. Some stand tall and stately, others short with bottlelike trunks. A few flaunt astonishing leaf patterns that look as if they were created by fashion designers.

The overall theme of this area is prosperity and business success. Fort Myers has a population of about 90,000, about the same as its sister city, Cape Coral. The island of Fort Myers Beach (pop. 14,000) fronts the city of Fort Myers and allows open access to the Gulf of Mexico, making it a popular place for homes with boat docks. The 7-mile-long island is tightly packed with small homes, condos, and beachfront properties. For being close to such a popular beach, prices are affordable, but winter traffic on the island can be horrific, and the number of tourists along the beachfront appalling. Be aware that the Fort Myers Beach population triples during the winter.

For quiet, rural island retirement, Pine Island could be your choice. Seventeen miles long and about 2 miles wide, this is the largest of the barrier islands in these parts. Its shores are almost completely ringed with mangrove estuaries, much of it dedicated as wildlife preserves. As its name indicates, the island is rustic, covered with pines, and it offers inexpensive retirement housing. Approximately 8,000 year-round residents are joined by another 4,000 during the winter months.

Pine Island is accessed from Cape Coral via a fishing bridge that crosses over to Matlacha and Little Pine Islands. This is known as "Florida's Fishingest Bridge"—at almost any time, day or night, you are apt to see fishermen dipping their lines into Matlacha Pass. This area is a throwback to the time when tiny fishing villages were the norm along Florida's southwest coast. The western shore sits in the lee of Captiva Island, which makes the water safe for sailing and peaceful fishing.

Fort Myers Climate

	Jan.	April	July	Oct.	Average Annual Rain	Snow
Daily Highs	74°	85°	91°	85°	54"	0
Daily Lows	53°	62°	74°	68°		

For more information contact Fort Myers Chamber of Commerce, 13601 McGregor Boulevard, Suite 15, Fort Myers, FL 33919; (239) 931-0931; www.lee chamber.com.

JACKSONVILLE, FLORIDA

Situated on the Atlantic coast in the northern part of the state, Jacksonville (pop. 750,000) experienced one of the fastest job growth rates in the Southeast, for years maintaining a 3.3 percent growth in its work force of 500,000. Jacksonville's major employment is in the service, finance, retail, insurance, and real-estate industries. Two major naval installations, the Jacksonville Air Station and the

Mayport Naval facility, contribute positively to the economy, and thousands of military retirees live in the area.

This part of Florida's east coast offers a mild climate year-round. The city seems almost surrounded by water, with the wide St. Johns River twisting about in the form of a horseshoe, about 20 miles of inter-coastal waterway, and uncounted miles of nearby ocean beach. As expected, many of Jacksonville's recreational activities are water-related. In addition to saltwater fishing and boating, several freshwater streams and lakes offer great fishing.

Although Jacksonville has its share of expensive golf course developments, gated communities, and posh neighborhoods, the overall quality of housing reflects the needs and purchasing ability of the area's large working middle class. Quality homes are widely available at very affordable prices. The median sales price of real estate is almost 15 percent below the national average. The cost of living is also made favorable by utility costs that are 18 percent lower than average and medical care costs 12 percent below average.

Jacksonville Climate

	Jan.	April	July	Oct.	Average Annual Rain	Snow
Daily Highs	65°	80°	91°	80°	53"	0
Daily Lows	42°	56°	72°	59°		

For more information contact Jacksonville Chamber of Commerce, 3 Independent Drive, Jacksonville, FL 32202; (904) 366-6600; www.myjaxchamber.com.

MIAMI AND FLORIDA'S GOLD COAST

Miami's boom started in the 1920s and spilled from Key Biscayne north to Fort Lauderdale, Pompano Beach, Boca Raton, all the way to Palm Beach and beyond. This is Florida's fabulous Gold Coast. A drive along the coastal streets and highways will explain how the Gold Coast received its name. It certainly took a lot of gold to build it, and more to maintain it.

Individually, the cities from West Palm Beach down to Coral Gables don't appear to be particularly large. Miami has only 360,000 people, North Miami Beach about 40,000, and West Palm Beach only about 79,000. But, together, more than 40 towns make up one long, enormous metropolitan area of almost three million people. With this many communities, there's no possibility of having a central focus, or a common downtown area. Broken into a string of suburbs, each town has its own shopping centers, stores, business districts, and an individual political reality. In this unconsolidated manner, Florida's Gold Coast resembles the Los Angeles sprawl.

Except for the classy sections along the beaches, most housing is in the form of single-family bungalows, low-profile condominiums, and expansive apartment complexes. In some of the less intensely developed areas, where things aren't so tightly packed, it's easy to forget that you are part of an urban sprawl. People commonly don't leave to go shopping away from their area; they have no need to. Each neighborhood is pretty much self-contained for shopping and services.

Florida's Gold Coast presents a fascinating series of contrasts, from tall forests of condominiums and apartment buildings reminiscent of New York's Park Avenue to rows of tract houses reminiscent of Los Angeles. Every imaginable type of housing and neighborhoods—all within miles or sometimes yards of each other—make for an interesting mixture. Sometimes, just 10 to 20 miles to the inland, the countryside can be totally uninhabited, the exclusive domain of alligators, deer, and mosquitoes.

The Florida Gold Coast is the part of the

state that you usually read about in your newspaper's travel section, the Florida you see on television and in movies. For some folks the thought of living in such a crowded area is a turnoff. But for others, the amenities of a metropolitan area—combined with a mild climate and gorgeous beaches—add up to ideal retirement living. They adore everything about the Gold Coast. They love the convenience of well-stocked shopping centers, good medical facilities, and a choice of good restaurants. Folks here enjoy apartment living, having someone else wash windows, mow lawns, and trim shrubs. As one lady put it, "We've lived all our lives in or near Manhattan. We couldn't survive in some dinky, one-horse town where they roll up the sidewalks after dark!"

Curiously, in the midst of this densely packed, tropical replica of Manhattan, distinct concepts of neighborhood and community emerge. We've visited several large condominium developments and are always fascinated by the way folks create their own islands of interests and community. A typical complex in Pompano Beach has a dozen eight-story buildings set apart in a parklike setting. Each building has complete laundry facilities and an exercise room. Jogging paths, swimming pools, and tennis courts are strategically placed about the grounds, and a clubhouse dominates the center.

In effect, the development corresponds to a small town or an intimate neighborhood in a larger city. The condo owners' association substitutes for city politics back home. Residents have a great time voting for officers, running for election, lobbying for pet projects, or trying to recall those who aren't doing their job. "I feel like I have a hell of a lot more control and say-so about my neighborhood now than I ever could hope for back in New York," said one resident who was in the middle of a fight

to redecorate the clubhouse and install more outdoor lighting.

As in any metropolitan area, living in the Gold Coast area has drawbacks. Higher crime rates, traffic jams, and crowded stores are pretty much standard. However, the crime picture is somewhat distorted in the Miami area because of certain, isolated neighborhoods with a vigorous commerce in illegal drugs and gang activities. Retired couples we've interviewed in the Gold Coast area tell us they feel just as safe in their neighborhoods as they did where they lived before retirement.

Miami and Florida's Gold Coast Climate

	Jan.	April	July	Oct.	Average Annual Rain	Snow
Daily Highs	75°	82°	89°	84°	60"	0
Daily Lows	56°	65°	74°	70°		

For more information contact Greater Miami Chamber of Commerce, Omni International Complex, 1601 Biscayne Boulevard, Miami, FL 33132-1260; (305) 350–7700; www.greatermiami.com.

PORTLAND, MAINE

Despite our habitual avoidance of cold-weather localities, we discovered that we really liked Portland. Its location on the ocean tends to keep the extreme cold away, although there does seem to be a lot of snow in the winter. Winters here are often described as being "mild by regional standards," although the standards inland can be somewhat harsh.

Our introduction to Portland and other Maine towns to the north came during a retirement seminar conducted by the American Association of Retirement Communities. Delegates from Maine chambers of commerce met to discuss the strategy and mechanics of publicizing their communities and convincing retired couples to take up residence. We were impressed by the sincerity of the delegates and by the towns they represented. Before and after the conference, we visited several ocean-front communities and liked what we saw. One interesting revelation for us was the number of retirees in Maine from New York and New Jersey, who made their relocation decisions because they had traditionally taken summer vacations in Maine and knew they liked it. I suppose those who took their vacations in the winter and traveled to Florida are living in Miami.

Portland is a combination of a laid-back small city and a hustling hub of economic activity, a place the city fathers refer to as "Maine's economic engine" or "the economic center of northern New England." The state's largest city (even though the population is only 65,000), Portland supports a surprising number of highly successful industries, including high-tech as well as traditional businesses that furnish a wide range of employment for those who might want to relocate for job change. Fishing is, of course, a big income producer here. Boston is only two hours away, for those who enjoy visiting a bigger city from time to time, for baseball, performing arts, and great restaurants.

Some of New England's finest ski resorts are within a two-hour drive of Portland, and, of course, outdoor adventures such as hiking, kayaking, biking, and rafting can be done a few miles from home, any time you care to go. Because of Portland's popularity, its charm, and its access to fresh lobster, the housing market can be tight. (Actually, fresh lobster has nothing to do with housing, but it's difficult to write about Maine without thinking of lobster.) Apartment vacancy rates are low, and property taxes can be high compared with the rest of the state. This demand in housing, however, has helped spawn the reha-

bilitation of many older buildings, giving some older charmers a new lease on life.

Portland Climate

	Jan.	April	July	Oct.	Average Annual Rain	Snow
Daily Highs	32°	52°	75°	59°	46"	37"
Daily Lows	14°	34°	55°	38°		

For more information contact Greater Portland Chamber of Commerce, 60 Pearl Street, Portland, ME 04101; (207) 772–2811; www.portlandregion.com.

RALEIGH, NORTH CAROLINA, AND THE UNIVERSITY TRIANGLE

Between the flat coastal regions of the mid-Atlantic and the Appalachians, a stretch of hardwood forests and gently rolling farmland host country villages, small towns, and sophisticated cities. The countryside is called the Midlands because it separates the flat coastal plain that slopes toward the Atlantic Ocean from the high Appalachian plateau in the west. The Midlands terrain is too rolling to be considered plains, yet not hilly enough to be foothills. The Midlands presents a unique combination of cultural choices: from Beethoven to bluegrass and from stock car racing to scholarly research. Just about any kind of intellectual and recreational pursuit imaginable can be found here.

Because three of North Carolina's top universities are clustered here in the Midlands, in three of the state's best-known cities, the region around Chapel Hill, Durham, and Raleigh is properly known as the University Triangle. Chapel Hill is home of the University of North Carolina, Duke University is located in Durham, and North Carolina State University is in Raleigh. Besides the three major universities found here, there are five four-year colleges and eight two-year colleges grouped within a few miles of one another, with more than 64,000 students in attendance.

Unlike some sections of the South, where outsiders are rare curiosities, the universities and the numerous research labs, think tanks, and other scientific endeavors recruit people from all over North America. It's claimed that per capita, more academics, Ph.Ds, and scientists live in the Triangle region than in any other part of the country. This is probably the "least Southern" place in the Carolinas and certainly in the South. Finding neighbors from your old hometown is highly possible. Because of the vast number of employment opportunities in the high-tech field, this area is a popular retirement destination for engineers, electronics technicians, and computer experts. Part-time work and consulting jobs are there for those who do not view retirement as a career in itself.

Raleigh (pop. 240,000) is North Carolina's state capital and the largest city in the Triangle. The combined population of the three cities is fast approaching the one-million mark, yet being spread over three locations, the population density appears to be lower than you might expect.

Home prices are higher than in most other North Carolina cities, which is understandable given the favorable economy and higher wages. The quality of housing is also well above average, yet for folks from some higher-priced areas of the country, prices look great. We interviewed a couple who moved to Raleigh after leaving a small apartment in New York City and buying a spacious five-bedroom home on two acres of wooded grounds. "Our entire apartment could fit into our new living room and kitchen," they said. "And never in our wildest dreams could we have afforded to buy our own apartment in New York City!" Because they bought when interest rates bottomed out, the monthly mortgage payments are one-third what they paid in rent for a tiny apartment.

Chartered in 1789 as the nation's first state university, the University of North Carolina has helped Chapel Hill to retain the essence of what a true college town should look like. Because the population of Chapel Hill is only around 49,000, the university's 23,000 students, 1,800 professors, and numerous support personnel exert an enormous influence on the cultural and recreational lives of the town's inhabitants. The downtown setting is user-friendly, with a laid-back pace one would expect from a place that hosts a world-class university. The school is set on a 687-acre campus that is as beautiful as the institution is prestigious. The city's residential neighborhoods seem to compete with the school's famous landscaping in beautifying Chapel Hill.

Medical care in Durham is as good as it gets. In fact Durham likes to call itself the "City of Medicine" because of its medical school and hospital. It used to be nicknamed "Tobacco Town" because tobacco money founded Duke University—but that name seems to be politically incorrect today. This is a larger city, with a population of about 187,000. Duke University's two impressive campuses also influence the community, not only financially but also culturally. Whether it's black-tie or blue jeans, ballet or beach music, the entire area has something for everyone. Duke's cultural programs amount to an astounding 500 presentations a year, most of them free to the general public.

Raleigh and the University Triangle Climate

	Jan.	April	July	Oct.	Average Annual Rain	Snow
Daily Highs	50°	72°	88°	72°	42"	8"
Daily Lows	29°	47°	67°	48°		

For more information contact Greater Raleigh Chamber of Commerce, 800 South Salisbury Street, Raleigh, NC 27601; (919)

664-7000; www.raleighchamber.org; or Durham Chamber of Commerce, 101 East Morgan Street, Durham, NC 27702; (919) 682-2133; www.durhamchamber.org.

SAVANNAH, GEORGIA

Savannah was the first British settlement in what is now the state of Georgia. It was founded in 1733, when General James Edward Oglethorpe selected the location on a bluff overlooking the Savannah River. Savannah's historic city hall occupies the spot where the British first landed. Instead of allowing a traditional, haphazard village layout to develop, Savannah was designed with a system of street grids, broken by a series of public squares. This was the country's first planned city, a masterpiece of urban design. Today the city is tastefully landscaped with live oaks, azaleas, fountains, and statues that give Savannah the charming flavor that sets the city apart as unique as well as beautiful. The downtown historic district (the largest of its kind in the country) has been not only restored but also made exceptionally livable.

Savannah's population today is about 132,000, with another 150,000 in its metropolitan area. The city is surrounded by some very livable communities, quite suitable for relocation, convenient to the city's historic center and shopping, and with very short commuting distances. Savannah is home to the Hunter Army Airfield and Fort Stewart military bases. The combined military installations employ more than 42,000 people and generate an annual federal expenditure of $1.4 billion, much of that going into Savannah's economy.

The Savannah area's range of real estate varies from exceptionally expensive properties on Skidaway Island, where building lots may run into six-figure prices, to livable neighborhoods in nearby towns, where acceptable places can be purchased for less than $100,000. One of Savannah's fastest-growing residential areas is on the fringes of the south side, only 6 miles from the historic district. A collection of attractive neighborhoods offer quality single-family housing, as well as a number of apartment complexes, townhouses, and shopping centers. To zip downtown is a matter of minutes.

Eighteen miles east of downtown Savannah, Tybee Island is the prototype of a summer beach community. People from Savannah and tourists from all over come here to enjoy sunning and shell collecting on the island's 2 miles of white sand beaches on the Atlantic. However, the 3,000 year-round residents enjoy the vacation atmosphere all year long. Accommodations are divided into short-term rentals of condos and apartments and permanent-resident housing, which tends to be older and not fancy. Other island communities on the way to Tybee Island are Wilmington, Whitemarsh, and Talahi. Like most Georgian islands, they are not crowded and have several nice-looking developments.

Home-owning retirees living in the county are beneficiaries of a local referendum passed in 2000 that prevents long-time residents from being taxed out of their dwellings. The legislation places a freeze on their property taxes by automatically raising homestead exemptions to match increases in values for as long as the resident owns and lives in the home.

Savannah Climate

	Jan.	April	July	Oct.	Average Annual Rain	Snow
Daily Highs	60°	78°	91°	78°	50"	0
Daily Lows	38°	54°	72°	56°		

For more information contact Savannah Chamber of Commerce, 101 East Bay Street, Savannah, GA 31401; (912) 644-6400; www.savannahchamber.com.

GLOSSARY

Agreement of sale—The legal contract between the buyer and seller of a property, including sale price, conditions, and settlement date.

Appraisal—An expert evaluation of the fair market value of a property, usually for tax or sale purposes.

Appreciation—An increase in the value of a property.

Buyer agent—An agent hired and paid for by the buyer of a property to negotiate the purchase.

Closing—The time when legal title to a property passes from seller to buyer; also known as settlement.

Closing costs—Costs incurred, usually by the buyer, regarding the sale of a property.

Curb appeal—Outside appearance of a house that arouses immediate interest and attraction.

Deed—Legal paper that proves ownership (title) of a property.

Depreciation—A decrease in the value of a property.

Easement—The right to enter or use a portion of another's land for a specific purpose.

Earnest money—The deposit given to the seller by the buyer to show serious intent to purchase.

Escrow—Something put in the care of a third party until certain conditions are fulfilled, such as a deed or money.

Floater—An insurance policy covering movable property regardless of its location at the time of loss or damage.

Home inspection—A professional service in which an expert examines a home's foundation, roof, plumbing, and electrical system, as well as its general condition inside and outside.

Home warranty—A protection plan for the repair or replacement of defective merchandise or workmanship.

Lien—A legal notice of the right of a lien holder (such as a mortgage lender) to be paid from the proceeds of a sale of property on which the lien was recorded.

Living will—A document, legal in some states, directing that all measures to support life be ended if the signer should be dying of an incurable condition.

Mortgage—A legal document representing a loan of money in return for the pledge of property as collateral for repayment of the loan with interest.

Multiple Listing Service (MLS)—A service in which property listings of member real estate agents are made available for all agents to sell.

Point—An amount equal to 1 percent of a loan secured by a mortgage. One or more points may be paid in advance by the borrower.

Power of attorney—A written statement legally authorizing a person to act for another.

Real estate agent—An employee of a real estate broker who has passed an exam and is licensed by the state to sell property.

Real estate broker—A person who has passed an advanced exam and is licensed to show properties to potential buyers, negotiate sales, and receive payment for these services.

Realtor—A registered collective membership mark that identifies a real estate professional who is a member of the National Association of Realtors and subscribes to its strict Code of Ethics.

Zoning district—Areas of a city or township that are divided into sections as determined by specific allowed uses for a property within that section, such as residential or commercial.

INDEX

ABOUT THE AUTHORS

Beverly Roman is a recognized expert in the field of relocation. She is the publisher of BR Anchor Publishing, which produces relocation books for all ages, and has written more than twenty books, the *Relocation Today* newsletter, and articles for national and local publications. A guest on radio and television shows, including ABC TV's *Home Show,* The Discovery Channel's *Home Matters,* and CNN's *Parenting Today*, she gained relocation expertise from her own eighteen moves, both domestically and internationally, with a family of five. She and her husband, Stan, live in Wilmington, North Carolina.

John Howells is a travel and feature writer who has written and co-authored several books about retirement, including *Where to Retire, Choose Costa Rica, Choose Mexico,* and *Retirement on a Shoestring.* He also writes articles about retirement and travel for magazines such as *Successful Retirement* and *International Living.* He has worked as a Linotype operator, an English teacher, and a silver miner. He and his wife live in Pacific Grove, California, and Costa Rica.